T0302229

THE DIGITALIZATION OF THE 21ST CENTURY SUPPLY CHAIN

The goal of this book is to gain a clear picture of the current status and future challenges with regard to the digitalization of the supply chain – from the perspective of the suppliers, the manufacturers, and the customers. They were the target groups of the book.

Digitization has touched upon all aspects of businesses, including supply chains. Technologies such as RFID, GPS, and sensors have enabled organizations to transform their existing hybrid (combination of paper-based and IT-supported processes) supply chain structures into more flexible, open, agile, and collaborative digital models. Unlike hybrid supply chain models, which have resulted in rigid organizational structures, unobtainable data, and disjointed relationships with partners, digital supply chains enable business process automation, organizational flexibility, and digital management of corporate assets.

In order to reap maximum benefits from digital supply chain models, it is important that companies internalize them as an integral part of the overall business model and organizational structure. Localized disconnected projects and silo-based operations pose a serious threat to competitiveness in an increasingly digital world.

The technologies discussed in this text – artificial intelligence, 3D printing, Internet of things, etc. – are beginning to come together to help digitize, automate, integrate, and improve the global supply chains. It's certainly an exciting and challenging time for both new supply chain professionals and long-time supply chain professionals.

Stuart M. Rosenberg is an accomplished supply chain management professional with a number of years of experience using outstanding communication and leadership skills to coach, mentor, and motivate professionals in challenging environments. As the president of First Choice

Supply Chain, his reputation as a savvy supply chain leader is beyond reproach for delivering resourceful business strategies and customer-focused solutions. His work with several worldwide corporations – Johnson & Johnson, Cadbury, Reckitt Benckiser, and Linde Gas, NA – and his far-reaching experience in launching, managing, and mentoring new programs and strategies resulted in greater customer confidence and improved business results. He has written and published numerous supply chain articles encompassing all disciplines of supply chain. In addition to his worldwide corporate experience, Stuart is an adjunct professor of supply chain at Brookdale Community College and Hudson Community College. Stuart also sits as an advisory board member at Seton Hall University's Stillman School of Business. He lives with his wife and son in New Jersey.

THE DIGITALIZATION OF THE 21ST CENTURY SUPPLY CHAIN

Stuart M. Rosenberg

Routledge
Taylor & Francis Group

LONDON AND NEW YORK

First published 2021
by Routledge
2 Park Square, Milton Park, Abingdon, Oxon OX14 4RN

and by Routledge
52 Vanderbilt Avenue, New York, NY 10017

Routledge is an imprint of the Taylor & Francis Group, an informa business

British Library Cataloguing-in-Publication Data
A catalogue record for this book is available from the British Library

Library of Congress Cataloging-in-Publication Data
Names: Rosenberg, Stuart, author.
Title: The digitalization of the 21st century supply chain/Stuart M. Rosenberg.
Description: Milton Park, Abingdon, Oxon; New York, NY: Routledge, 2021. | Includes bibliographical references and index. | Identifiers: LCCN 2020021898 (print) | LCCN 2020021899 (ebook) | ISBN 9780367516789 (hardback) | ISBN 9781003054818 (ebook)
Subjects: LCSH: Business logistics–Information technology. | Inventory control–Data processing.
Classification: LCC HD38.5 .R6733 2021 (print) | LCC HD38.5 (ebook) | DDC 658.70285–dc23
LC record available at https://lccn.loc.gov/2020021898
LC ebook record available at https://lccn.loc.gov/2020021899

ISBN: 978-0-367-51678-9 (hbk)
ISBN: 978-1-003-05481-8 (ebk)

Typeset in Bembo
by Deanta Global Publishing Services, Chennai, India

CONTENTS

INTRODUCTION

The future is now

In the 21st century, supply chain management professionals must have an array of skills to be successful, including mathematics, logistics, basic engineering, and most importantly, people skills. Supply chain is about creative, real-time problem solving. Supply chain calls for an understanding of the fine distinctions in global markets to be successful.

Continuous process improvement begets greater efficiency and profitability – from supply chain planning through execution.

In almost every industry, the marketplace is becoming more competitive and demanding. There is more pressure than ever before to do more for less.

That climate should encourage executives to closely examine every aspect of their supply chain. A recent study showed companies with a group dedicated to supply chain optimization were almost twice as likely to reach their revenue and margin goals as those without such a focus. That examination should be guided by the fundamentals of continuous process improvement (CPI), which describes an ongoing process to strengthen any aspect of your daily operations. From supply chain planning through execution, continuous process improvement has proven to be an avenue to greater efficiency and profitability.

CPI impacts the three main aspects of a supply chain: people, processes, and technology. First, employees must be in a position that takes complete advantage of their individual skill sets and strengths. Second, an organization must identify the best path(s) to reach its goals. Finally, the business must employ the latest technological solutions to boost efficiency and meet customer demand, all without increasing expenses.

CPI is not something with only theoretical appeal. Once implemented company wide, companies have real and lasting results. Included in this are improved bottom lines and an employee-engaged workforce that drives productivity and brings positive cultural change.

There are four basic steps: identify, plan, execute, and review. It starts with identifying the processes that are hindering the bottom line or preventing new business. Speak with all stakeholders, from workers on the floor to the operations team to the IT staff. Brainstorm ideas. Transparency and communication is the key – everyone must be aware of what changes are coming, why, and who is leading each initiative.

Following this, develop a plan prioritizing the tasks that provide a clear return on investment. A cause-and-effect matrix may help you find the most pressing areas of improvement for your organization.

The third step is execution. Not surprisingly, this is the most difficult part of implementing CPI. You know what needs to change but making that happen can be an immense challenge. This should be a bump in the road (rather than a roadblock) if you strike the right balance between priorities and available resources. Choose the systems development lifecycle that works best for you. Think about how much training is involved. Consider the details of deployment. Plan for success. For example, you may first deploy these changes at distribution centers near your support staff.

Finally, review the effects of the change. This may be a relatively simple process for small- and mid-sized companies, while enterprise-level businesses may need a more formal procedure. It's critical to collect feedback from the people on the floor who use the processes and technologies every day. Their input should guide your next CPI cycle.

Looking beyond any technological systems, logistical infrastructure and analytics considerations must not overlook and cannot overemphasize the importance of an engaged, committed workforce for increased productivity in your supply chain.

It's important to foster communication within the supply chain, and maintain it for the long term, with a high expectation for improvement. Continuous education among employees and management is vital to the improvement of processes, products, and services. A performance-driven culture will result in maximized savings, improved service levels, and a motivated team of gifted employees.

Part 1

LEAN AND SUPPLY CHAIN MANAGEMENT PRINCIPLES

Lean is a methodology that changes the philosophy and culture of an organization. For more than 50 years, organizations have invested time and money adopting the principles of Lean (while originating at Toyota Corporation for manufacturing operations, the principles of Lean have since spread to many types of businesses and functional areas).

The focus of Lean is to maximize quality, minimize unnecessary steps, and optimize customer value. A Lean organization focuses on providing the best quality within the shortest possible lead time, while minimizing waste throughout your processes (waste being classified as any resource that is not being used properly). We may first think that minimizing waste means minimizing inventory, but time, effort, and people are also resources to be utilized properly. Analyzing how people are used and time is spent is a critical step in minimizing waste.

Lean supply chain management requires businesses to examine every process in their supply chain and identify areas that are using unnecessary resources, which can be measured in dollars, time, or raw materials. The analysis can improve a company's competitiveness, its customer service, and its overall profitability.

1

INTRODUCTION TO LEAN AND SUPPLY CHAIN PRINCIPLES

When properly implemented, Lean can have an all-encompassing influence in the modern organization. Unfortunately, that is not always the case as management is not fully aware of all the uses this continuous improvement methodology offers. This chapter will describe the full definition of Lean and supply chain principles for which the two can and should be fettered together. This can be used by either the director of supply chain or the head of operations as a guide to develop the supply chain role.

Lean supply chain management represents a new way of thinking about supplier networks. Lean principles require cooperative supplier relationships while balancing cooperation and competition. Cooperation involves a spectrum of collaborative relationships and coordination mechanisms. Supplier partnerships and strategic alliances represent a key feature of Lean supply chain management.

Lean is a concept, a philosophy, a practice, and a set of tools, all wrapped in one. For more than 50 years, organizations have invested time and money adopting the principles of Lean (while they originated at Toyota Corporation for manufacturing operations, the principles of Lean have since spread to many types of businesses and functional areas).

The focus of Lean is to maximize quality, minimize unnecessary steps or waste, and optimize customer value (provide them what they want when they want it). The two primary principles of Lean, just in time and Jidoka, are referred to as the foundation of the Lean culture.

A Lean organization focuses on providing the best quality within the shortest possible lead time, while minimizing waste throughout its processes (waste being classified as any resource that is not being used properly). We may first think that mitigating waste means minimizing inventory, but time, effort, and people are also resources to be utilized properly. Analyzing how people are used and time is spent is a critical step in minimizing waste.

Lean principles and culture can be applied to supply chain planning, the biggest objectives of which are to reduce costs and improve customer service. A sequence of conceptual tools evolved from the Toyota Production System that can be applied to supply chain planning. Let's take a look at a few and see how they can help organizations become Lean.

Just in time (JIT) ensures all efforts are directed at providing only the goods and services required by customers, both when they want it and in the exact quantity they desire. The goals of JIT are aligned with the goals of supply chain planning.

Value stream mapping involves mapping out all the steps of your processes, including the flow, timing of each step, and wait times for all associated activities. Value stream mapping identifies and eliminates waste. There is no doubt that mapping out the various processes in supply chain planning and how they are all connected will lead to a better understanding of the value of each step and how to streamline and eliminate non-value-added activities.

Kaizen (continuous improvement) is an ongoing process of looking for improvements in every area of the process. This philosophy can be embraced at all levels of the organization and applied to any task. Finding ways to do things more efficiently, accurately, and effectively minimizes waste and adds value to supply chain planning processes. Doing more with less is all about finding ways to minimize waste and improve efficiencies.

5S stands for **Sort, Straighten, Standardize, Shine,** and **Sustain**. This five-step process organizes all areas of the workplace. The **Sort** process consists of distinguishing needed tools from unneeded tools and eliminating clutter. **Straighten** is the concept of keeping everything in the correct place to allow for easy access. **Shine** focuses on keeping the workplace neat and clean. **Standardizing** is the process of making the previous three steps habitual. **Sustain** is the concept of keeping and maintaining established procedures for every function and step of the operation. Substitute 'data and software' for 'solutions' and you can see how 5S could apply to supply chain planning.

The Five Whys is the philosophy of always asking questions. Small children love to ask 'why?'. Asking questions leads to an understanding of how things work and to finding potential fixes for problems. This should be a core principle in supply chain planning. Determining why something happened in the supply chain leads to the ability to anticipate and optimally respond.

Are you using Lean principles in your supply chain organization?

2

JUST-IN-TIME

A JIT (just-in-time) system is an inventory management philosophy aimed at reducing waste and redundant inventory by delivering products, components, or materials just when an organization needs them. There is immense interest from the supply chain community on how it in overall inventory management system; therefore, I thought to expand on this topic.

It is a well-known fact that the JIT system was developed by the Toyota Motor Company during the 1950s and 1960s. The philosophy of the JIT system is that parts and materials should be supplied at the very moment they are needed in the factory production process. Here are five significant features of the JIT system you might find useful:

- There are three JIT system principles.
- There are six inventory management principles.
- There are implications for logistics integration.
- There are benefits for implementing a JIT system in an organization.
- There are some problems with implementing a JIT system.

The three JIT improvements can only become available with efficient supply chains. There are three JIT system principles which are of importance when considering implementation. The JIT system focuses on improving the efficiency of material processes, and quality is very important. The JIT system focuses on improving the effectiveness of processes and operations that add value to the materials. Inventory is considered as waste and should be reduced as much as possible. The company's employees are its most valuable resource. It is essential that everyone understands the JIT system and gets involved with making it a success.

Mitigating waste is one of the basic aims of the JIT system. This requires the effective management of inventory throughout the entire supply chain. A manufacturing firm will initially seek to reduce inventory and improve operations within its own organization. It is also vital to an organization that improvements are carried out continuously to enable it to maintain competitiveness. This is in line with the concept of continuous improvement. In an attempt to minimize waste attributed to inefficient inventory management, six principles related to JIT have been identified through the implementation of Lean. They are the following:

- Reduce lot size and increase frequency of orders.
- Reduce buffer inventory.
- Reduce purchasing cost.
- Improve material handling.
- Seek zero inventories.
- Seek reliable suppliers.

Although the application of JIT has been concentrated on manufacturing operations, material handling and storage, and supplier deliveries, its principles can be extended throughout the supply chain. JIT methods have proven quite successful in simplifying and streamlining the material supply chain and the information flows which plan and control it. JIT has a number of implications for supply chain logistics:

- Transportation becomes an even more vital element of logistics under a JIT system. This means supply chains need shorter, more consistent transit times and more sophisticated communications.

- Proper implementations of JIT require that the firm fully integrate all logistics activities. Many tradeoffs are required, but without the coordination provided by integrated logistics management, JIT cannot be fully implemented.
- Warehousing assumes an expanded role of consolidation of facility instead of storage facility.

As with any system or methodology that is being planned, there are pros and cons. Just-in-time is no exception.

JIT produces benefits for firms in four major areas: improved inventory turns, better customer service, decreased warehouse space, and improved response time. Other specific benefits are: productivity improvements and greater control between various production stages; diminished raw materials, work in progress, and finished goods inventory; a reduction in manufacturing cycle times; dramatically improved inventory turnover rates; reduced distribution costs; lower transportation costs; improved quality of supplier products; and reduced number of transportation carriers and suppliers.

Not all organizations find it suitable. The JIT system has three inherent problems which need to addressed and supervised:

1. Supplier production schedules: JIT depends on a supplier's ability to provide parts in accordance with the firm's production schedule. Smaller, more frequent orders can result in higher ordering costs. Furthermore, as a large number of parts are produced in small quantities, suppliers may incur higher production and setup costs.
2. Level production schedules: JIT is difficult to implement with uneven demand and does require level production schedules. If your business operates in a high demand-variation environment, then JIT is not for you!
3. Supplier locations: JIT is not suitable for long-distance suppliers. As the distance between the firm and its supplier increases, delivery times may become more erratic and less predictable, and short, frequent deliveries may not be practical.

The just-in-time manufacturing system has long been an integral part of supply chain management. It plays a vital role in enhancing the supply chain processes of any company and is very important to be looked upon in a very careful manner. In this literary review, we will also look at the role of JIT in the supply chain from three perspectives: quality, buyer–supplier relationship, and customer relationship.

JIT systems are very important tools for companies to ensure **quality** improvements. The just-in-time environment helps in increasing the quality at almost all stages in a supply chain. I am speaking about vendor quality, product quality, design quality, and manufacturing workmanship. Therefore, quality of the entire supply chain improves.

Just-in-time inventory management is essentially a function of 'pull systems' in which goods are delivered only when they are needed, but they have to be delivered on time. The research tells how far the **buyer** and **supplier** should go in terms of finding out how much and at what point in time should they be delivered with goods. The suppliers and manufacturers should be flexible in the order quantities, hence maintaining the required level of inventory.

In order to bring this relationship to fruition, there must be mutual trust, open communication, transparency, and partnership. The balance of power in a buyer–supplier relationship is very delicate, and organizational strategies should aim to maintain that balance of power. Flexibility from both parties is required, especially when there are issues in quantity and delivery frequency .

Just-in-time can be adapted to other areas of the supply chain, including manufacturing, procurement, warehousing and distribution, and demand planning. Below, we will see how they all tie into just-in-time inventory management.

Just-in-time manufacturing

Just-in-time manufacturing has transformed manufacturing methods in some industries. By relying on daily deliveries of most supplies, it eliminates waste due to overproduction and lowers warehousing costs. Supplies are closely monitored and quickly altered to meet changing demands, and small and accurate resupply deliveries must be made just as they are needed. Because there are no spares, the components must be free of defects. Plants wholly dedicated to the JIT concept require a logistics staff to schedule production, balancing product demand with plant capacity and availability of inputs. JIT has worked most effectively for large automobile manufacturers, who may have several thousand suppliers feeding parts into 100 factories that assemble components for 20 assembly lines.

To elaborate further, under just-in-time manufacturing, actual orders dictate what should be manufactured, so that the exact quantity is produced at the exact time that is required. Just-in-time manufacturing goes hand in hand with continuous improvement.

Just-in-time production requires intricate planning in terms of procurement policies and the manufacturing process if its implementation is to be a success. Highly advanced technological support systems provide the necessary back-up that just-in-time manufacturing demands, with production scheduling software and electronic data interchange being the most sought after.

Like any concept, theory, or methodology, there are advantages and disadvantages to the implementation of JIT. Below is a list of both.

Advantages:

- Just-in-time manufacturing keeps stock holding costs to a bare minimum. The release of storage space results in better utilization of space and thereby bears a favorable impact on the rent paid and on any insurance premiums that would otherwise need to be made.
- Just-in-time manufacturing eliminates waste, as out-of-date or expired products do not enter into this equation at all.
- As under this technique only essential stocks are obtained, less working capital is required to finance procurement. Here, a minimum reorder level is set, and only once that mark is reached, fresh stocks are ordered, making this a boon to inventory management too.
- Due to the aforementioned low level of stocks held, the organization's return on investment (referred to as ROI in management parlance) would generally be high.

Disadvantages:

- Just-in-time manufacturing provides zero tolerance for mistakes, as it makes reworking very difficult in practice, as inventory is kept to a bare minimum.

- There is a high reliance on suppliers, whose performance is generally outside the purview of the manufacturer.
- As there are no buffers for delays, production downtime and line idling can occur, which would bear a detrimental effect on finances and on the equilibrium of the production process.
- The organization would not be able to meet an unexpected increase in orders due to the fact that there are no excess finished goods.

Thus, if your organization decides that just-in-time manufacturing fits best, these safeguards should be taken into consideration:
    Safeguards:

- Management buy-in and support at all levels of the organization are required if a just-in-time manufacturing system is to be successfully adopted.
- Adequate resources should be allocated, so as to obtain technologically advanced software that is generally required if a just-in-time system is to be successful.
- Building a close, trusting relationship with reputed and time-tested suppliers will minimize unexpected delays in the receipt of inventory.
- Just-in-time manufacturing cannot be adopted overnight. It requires commitment in terms of time, and adjustments to corporate culture would be required, as it is starkly different from traditional production processes.

Just-in-time manufacturing is a philosophy that has been successfully implemented in many manufacturing organizations. It is an optimal system that reduces inventory while being increasingly responsive to customer needs; this is not to say that it is not without its pitfalls. However, these disadvantages can be overcome with a little forethought and a lot of commitment at all levels of the organization.

Just-in-time procurement

Just-in-time procurement is a Lean purchasing strategy. You purchase goods so that they're delivered just as they're needed to meet customer demand. With JIT, when you get customer orders, you plan purchases.

You purchase the minimum number of items to meet customer demand. JIT purchasing typically results in smaller but more frequent deliveries.

The goal of JIT procurement is to reduce the carrying cost of inventory. Less inventory on hand means you pay less in storage and insurance costs. JIT also requires less cash in the short term.

There are several benefits to JIT procurement, but there are risks, too. You need to strategically manage the process carefully. If you don't, you may have stock outs. Stock outs can lead to lost business – both short-term and long-term. This strategy must include a fully integrated enterprise resource planning system that includes as one of its modules a materials requisition program.

Using technology can sharply reduce your ordering and carrying costs. Technology allows you to create and approve purchase orders, update your inventory records, and pay for inventory electronically. Technology also allows many firms to have access to real-time inventory quantities. This change reduces the number of hours your staff spends on inventory.

Another big factor is long-term contracts. If you contract long-term with a supplier, you lock in an inventory price and the amounts to be purchased over time. You eliminate price fluctuations, which makes planning easier. You may also be able to secure discounts by entering into a long-term contract. Other benefits, such as superior quality expectation and on-time delivery, are expected with a long-term contract.

Of course, it's important that the long-term contract provides enough inventories to meet your needs. If you need to buy more products over and above the supplier contract, you'll probably pay higher unit costs. That's because you may be buying at the last minute, and you'll also be buying a much smaller amount than what's in the contract. A supplier, therefore, is likely to demand a higher price for these 'extra' orders.

Here are earmarks to consider before implementing JIT procurement:

- Product sourcing and analysis: it involves determining the best materials for your business and the geographical location of those materials.
- Supplier identification and selection: there should be a robust process to choose the most beneficial supplier of your materials.
- Supplier performance evaluation: a firm should be frequently evaluating their supplier's ability to deliver materials at the right time, to the right place, and in the right amounts.

- Supplier sustainability issues: it involves questioning whether you have established sustainability guidelines for your suppliers that address issues such as environmental compliance, employment practices, and product and ingredient safety.

Part of the success of any JIT procurement system is supporting proactive suppliers who expedite orders, maintain inventories, and provide direct communication with the client. To get this commitment, a firm should develop long-term relationships and foster a service-level requirement which would create a win-win relationship.

Just-in-time logistics

Companies that are conducting business in the global economy are doing so in a continuously changing and increasingly competitive environment. They have started to pay special attention to their supply chain management in order to have sustainable competitiveness. Recently, logistics management has become an important tool to increase the competitiveness of companies. Logistics management can be defined as a part of the supply chain which plans, implements, and controls the efficient, effective forward and reverse flow and storage of goods, services, and related information between the point of origin and the point of consumption in order to meet customer requirements.

Just-in-time management, which was first applied by Toyota Corporation, involves the delivery of necessary goods to the production line just in time without any raw materials storage. As a current concept, just-in-time logistics can be also defined as the application of the JIT management philosophy to four main components of logistics: customer services, order processing, inventory management, and transportation management. The aim of this section is to present the importance of just-in-time logistics for companies and discuss why it should be considered as a logistics strategy by companies. Waste elimination and improvement of service quality objectives of the JIT concept also relate to business logistics. Application of JIT philosophy to the logistics area results in several benefits such as determination of waste sources, increasing delivery speed of goods to customers, improvement of processes by organizing business requirements and manpower plans for logistics, and increasing accord between suppliers and customers.

Globalization is forcing firms to be more careful about customer satisfaction and profitability. Organizations must use different tools to develop loyal customers who are less sensitive to product price increases and help firms to increase profits. Logistics is one of the key tools that builds cost and service advantages to the firms.

JIT is a system that gets rid of some supplying, storing, and securing activities that were needed for manufacturing to save time and reduce the cost. It can be interpreted as a total materials management theory. JIT covers suppliers, customers, and manufacturers. JIT is a philosophy which encompasses almost all business processes and functions within the supply chain. Thus, just-in-time logistics is a natural outgrowth of just-in-time for inventory, procurement, and manufacturing.

In the 1990s, companies began to view logistics as more than simply a source of cost savings and to recognize it as a source of augmenting products or services offerings as a part of the broader supply chain process to create a competitive advantage. The Council of Logistics Management defines logistics as the process of planning, implementing, and storage of raw materials, in-process inventory, finished goods, and related information from the point of origin to the point of consumption for the purpose of meeting customer requirements. The general description of logistics in the literature is '7Rs', that is, the ability to deliver the Right products to the Right customer at the Right place, in the Right condition and Right quantity at the Right time, at the Right costs. Logistical activities serve as a link between production and consumption and provide a conduit between production and market locations or suppliers separated by distance and time. The operations which are coordinated by logistics can be listed as follows: planning and marketing strategy, market strategy and product design, production planning, materials management, inventory management, warehousing and materials handling, distribution, warehouse, and transportation.

As a new concept, just-in-time logistics can be defined as the application of the JIT management philosophy to four main components of logistics, including customer services, order processing, inventory management, and transportation management. If the flow of goods and services is well managed, the quality of customer service will increase.

Customer service is related to the output of logistics systems and plays a very important role in creating, developing, and maintaining customer loyalty and satisfaction. Order processing includes all the order activities, including collecting, checking, entering, and transmitting order information. It reflects a relationship between suppliers and firms. The order cycle time, that is, the time from when a customer transmits an order to the time the customer receives that order, is very crucial for customer satisfaction. The firms can compress the order cycle time by implementing just-in-time logistics successfully. Inventory management involves managing appropriate inventory levels, which is necessary to serve the demand in a supply chain. It means keeping stock levels as low as possible but at the same time providing the desired level of stock available to serve customers' demand. That will lead firms to significantly reduce logistics costs. Transportation transfers materials, components, and finished products between raw materials suppliers, distributors, retailers, and end customers in a supply chain.

There are three logistics activities in a firm's logistics supply chain. These three stages of logistics activities are inbound logistics (materials management), intra-plant logistics, and outbound logistics (physical distribution). As mentioned above, there are four main components of logistics, and each component takes place in a different logistics stage. While transportation management is placed in inbound logistics, order processing and inventory management are placed in intra-plant logistics, and finally, customer service is placed in outbound logistics. To attain the complete benefits of JIT, it should be implemented in all three logistics activities.

There is a very strong bond between inbound logistics and just-in-time. Just-in-time improves supplier operations, enhances transportation operations with respect to inbound carriers, reduces the level and improves the management of inventories, does not cause overall inbound logistics costs to increase, and increases the quality and performance of inbound logistics. JIT affects both the entire organization and the logistics function in particular. With the implementation of JIT, a number of managerial, operational, and organizational changes occur in inbound logistics such as purchasing. For example, criteria for supplier selection are anticipated to change, inbound shipment size is expected to decline, and paper work is expected to be reduced. In addition, it is suggested that these changes will result in specific logistics-related outcomes like the timely delivery of material to production and an overall decrease in logistics costs.

In addition, it can result in reduced inventory costs, shorter lead times, and improved productivity for buying organizations. Changes in inbound logistics with the implementation of JIT will of course affect outbound logistics outcomes such as the cost and percentage of on-time delivery. It may also have a direct impact on the inefficiencies associated with suppliers shipping smaller lot sizes, which increases the inbound logistics cost.

There is also a close relationship between intra-bound logistics and JIT application. JIT systems can be applied to internal business logistics because it is about both the process and the transfer of all required materials and products on time and to the desired place. Reducing waste and improving services are the goals of JIT, and these goals are relevant and applicable to internal business logistics as well. In internal business logistics, waste can be defined as anything other than the minimum amount of equipment, space, and workers' time. The firms can apply the philosophy of JIT to discover waste sources in the processes. Moreover, JIT can improve services by planning the manpower and facility requirements to meet the distribution needs, reducing product introduction time through responsive delivery, improving logistics service quality by forging supplier and customer partnerships, and so on. In the successful implementation of JIT into intra-bound logistics, employees are the key factor. They represent the core of the firm's capabilities. To reduce waste and improve services, firms need intellectual, skilled employees who are empathetic. Team work is another key factor for success. A team that consists of members from purchasing, materials control, process/design engineering, production, and suppliers can solve many quality problems in supplies and enable the firm to meet the market requirements better.

Customer service that is related to the final output is a critical element for outbound logistics. Customer service is not only about good service levels but also about the financial costs incurred from providing quality customer services, because minimizing costs is key to survival and prosperity in a competitive marketplace. As part of just-in-time logistics, the just-in-time fundamental objective is very simple: to satisfy the customer by delivering the right goods or services in the right quantities at the right times while minimizing total process cost by eliminating waste of all kinds from the supply chain.

There are some essential elements for the success of just-in-time logistics. For example, management support is the most important factor to make implementation efforts sustainable. Employee involvement and cooperation are certainly another important factor for success in JIT-L. Employee engagement improves the procurement lead-time performance. In the organization, creation of quality awareness is also necessary for incurring the full benefits of just-in-time logistics. A number of managerial, operational, and organizational changes in purchasing should also be made. Firms that would like to apply just-in-time logistics will reduce wastes and improve services in their logistics activities. As given in the definition of just-in-time, there are four core activities of logistics that just-in-time management philosophy can apply: customer services, order processing, inventory management, and transportation management. Creating, developing, and maintaining customer loyalty and satisfaction can be carried by the application of JIT-L to customer service. At the same time, firms can compress the order cycle time by implementing JIT-L successfully. Keeping stock levels as low as possible but also providing the desired level of stock available to serve customers' demand is inventory management's goal, which is achieved by JIT-L. Transportation management is another important activity in logistics. Improved transportation management may cause increased sales, increased market share, and ultimately increased profit growth.

3

VALUE STREAM MAPPING

Before we can delve into the workings of value stream mapping, we must have an understanding of what it is.

Value stream mapping is a Lean manufacturing technique, is very adaptable to supply chains, and is used to document, analyze, and improve the flow of information or materials required to produce a product or service for a customer. Value stream mapping is a drawing tool that helps you to **see** and understand the flow of material and information as a product or service makes its way through the value stream.

A value stream map takes into account not only the activity of the product but the management and information systems that support the basic process. This is especially helpful when working to reduce cycle time, because you gain insight into the decision-making flow in addition to the process flow.

A value stream map allows you to see a top-down overview of your business processes. Later, one can analyze the workflow, identifying wastes and inefficiencies. Typically, here are a few things you'd want to be on the lookout for:

- Delays that hold up the process
- Restraints that limit the process
- Excess inventory that ties up resources unproductively

The following tips will be required to start drawing *your* value stream map.

First up, you need to decide what you want to map. In some businesses, one value stream map can cover just about everything the company does. This is especially true if your company produces a single product.

If you have a complex mix of products or services, however, then you'd have to draw a separate map for each. With which process you'd start is, of course, up to you. Generally, though, you'd want to start off with the highest value areas.

To actually carry out the mapping, you'd want to gather a small project team consisting of representatives from different departments. They have a first-hand perspective on how things are done, and how well the current system works. You might even figure out several ways to improve the processes without even consulting the value stream map. Next, you will need a project manager. This could be a senior manager who understands value stream mapping, or you can get an external consultant to help you.

As you work, you will create your map – but be aware, changes are inevitable, as someone may just remember a missed step somewhere along the line, and that can change the whole picture.

To actually draw the map, you can use:

- Pen and paper – the simplest solution, just grab an A3 piece of paper and a pencil and get to work
- Flowchart software – dedicated tools used for all sorts of business process mapping
- Workflow management software – custom solutions for managing company workflows. In addition to simple mapping capabilities, you can also keep track of and manage the workflows

Now that you know the basics of value stream mapping, here are the exact steps you'd need to take to carry out the project. They will be discussed in further detail below.

1. Decide how far you want to go.
2. Define the steps.
3. Indicate the information flow.
4. Gather the critical data.
5. Add the data to the map.
6. Identify the seven wastes.
7. Create the 'new' value stream map.

Start your mapping by indicating a start and end point. This would show where your internal process begins and ends. Some companies, however, prefer to map out the entire value chain or supply chain, internal and external. The value stream map begins with the delivery of materials from direct suppliers and ends with delivery to the customer.

If your production processes are complex, you might decide to map each of the value-adding processes in greater detail after completing your overall map. In this case, you would start with the process that allocates the work as 'supplier' and the process that receives it as the 'client'.

Then, define or determine which steps in the process you need to map out. For a manufacturer it might look like this:

Receiving→Stow or Putaway→Pick→Production Floor→
Q.C.→Shipping or Warehouse

One of the important rewards of value stream mapping is that it includes information flows. The teams or individuals responsible for each process that takes the product from input to output also need information. Where does it come from and how is this information passed on? Perhaps our manufacturer has a centralized planning department which receives sales information and places orders with the suppliers. It then uses this info and provides a weekly or monthly schedule for each of the processes.

Add this department in the middle of the sheet between the input and the output blocks, draw another block below it to indicate the weekly plan, and draw arrows from the plan to each of the departments it informs.

Now that you have the nuts and bolts, an in-depth look at each process is required. Real or actual data is needed so some of your mapping team might have to spend a little time collecting the information you need. Typical details that require scrutiny include:

- The inventory items held for each process
- The cycle time (typically per unit)
- The transfer time
- The number of people needed to perform each step
- The number of products that must be scrapped
- The pack or pallet size that will be used
- The overall batch size that each step handles

Once all the information is collected, you can start adding it to your map. Draw a table or data box under each process. If you've used historical data, be sure to verify it using the current inputs and outputs for each process. Indicate the timeline involved in each process beneath your data blocks.

The following explains the method for constructing supply chain value stream mapping:

1. On a blank sheet of paper the manufacturer is placed in the center. The manufacturer is the core element of supply chain value stream mapping, because he is at the origin of the supply chain. He functions as a pivot for downstream and upstream in the supply chain. The manufacturer is represented by the factory symbol.
2. Suppliers related to the manufacturer are identified and drawn. Suppliers relate to the manufacturer with regard to information, material flow, and financial information. Suppliers have a direct impact on consistent product quality, volume compliance, and on-time delivery in relation to the final consumer. In order to draw the suppliers in their different tiers, the symbol of a large circle is used.
3. The distributors down to the end consumers are identified and drawn, representing the actors downstream in the supply chain. They are represented by large triangles.
4. The material flow is mapped. This is a necessary step in the supply chain to understand the path the materials take and the relationships

that exist between suppliers and distributors. It is represented by a large broad arrow.

5. Data regarding material flow is obtained and included. This activity identifies volume forecasts or volume of materials ordered in the purchase program (volume requested), as well as the volume received, i.e. the amount of material or raw material received at the warehouse (volume received). Finally, the time control variable is added as On-Time Delivery (OTD).

6. Mapping the information flow allows the identification of the path of the information which triggers the material flow from the supply chain. It is drawn as a thin continuous arrow.

7. The data from the information flow is obtained and included. This action identifies the delivery forecast of the purchase orders. The purchasing program called Schedule Delivery is used. In addition, data from the On-Time Delivery is obtained, which means the actual time in which the order was received at the warehouse.

The supply chain manager, with the help of these symbols, is able to quickly and easily determine the breach that exists in material and information flows in his supply chain. When this analysis has been completed, the operation manager can make an action plan for improvement to alleviate the detected breaks in the analyzed supply chain, both in material flow and in information flow.

This implementation will highlight the wasteful activities which need to be eliminated or mitigated and with this, how much production capacity will be 'opened'. Supply chain value stream mapping can be the tool with which to perform those functions. Additionally, the link between the supply chain and the principles of quality, continuous improvement, and Lean manufacturing can only be put into practice using techniques and tools that allow managers to apply them directly and easily. Below, at least four managerial implications are mentioned:

1. Quick and easy visualization of the company's supply chain. It can be performed both on paper and on an electronic device.

2. Ability to observe in detail the behavior of the supply chain regarding both material flow and information flow of critical components to be processed at the manufacturer's.

3. Prioritization and critical identification of disruptions and gaps in the supply chain regarding the competitive priorities volume and on-time delivery.
4. Creation of an action plan to improve both the relationships of the players in the supply chain and its continuous flow.

4

KAIZEN

Principles

Before we delve any further into Kaizen – philosophy, application, structure, examples, and the Kaizen way – we must define the term as clearly as humanly possible. *Kaizen* is a Japanese word meaning continuous improvement. It's made up of two characters in Japanese: *kai*, which means 'change', and *zen*, which means 'good'. It's used to describe a company culture where everyone, from the CEO to the front-desk clerk, regularly evaluates his or her work and thinks of ways to improve it. The concept is that small steps on a regular basis will lead to large improvements over time.

Kaizen is a slow but ongoing process of improvement, not a concentrated or quickly implemented set of changes. The improvements are suggested by the person doing the work as opposed to outside consultants. If a worker has a problem to address or is considering whether a change will make sense, he should pull in several team members for a quick discussion and brainstorming session and then decide what to do from there.

Kaizen is a way of thinking. It is a cultural change within the organization as opposed to one tool.

Practicing Kaizen means eliminating waste. Toyota's Taichi Ohno identified the 'eight wastes' of manufacturing as: *DOWNTIME*

- Defects
- Overproduction
- Waiting
- Non-Employee Utilization (Lack)
- Transportation
- Inventory
- Motion
- Excess Processing or Production

If a company is truly practicing Kaizen, every employee from the shop-floor worker to the CEO is working to eliminate waste on a daily basis.

But what is the best method of Kaizen for the entire supply chain? If within a single organization, we are asking each employee to think lean and to eliminate waste, then within the supply chain we must ask each organization to do the same. However, simply performing Kaizen within the individual departments comprising a company's supply chain is not sufficient. Not only must we ask them to begin practicing Kaizen *within their four walls*, but we must work on supply chain improvement as a whole. This is because there are often wastes within a supply chain that we can only see when we consider the entire supply chain rather than simply one department's process within it. So, we've determined that we need to *Kaizen* both the supply chain as a whole and the individual departments and processes within them. What are the tools that help us accomplish this?

1. Value stream mapping. Value stream mapping helps us to see the entire picture and identify changes (*kaizen*) that will improve the supply chain as a whole. Through VSM, we understand the sources of waste created within material and information flows.
2. Supplier associations. Supplier associations help improve communication and knowledge across a supply chain, thus enabling Kaizen throughout the supply chain.

3. Kaizen Events. Kaizen Events can help us implement improvements to particular points within the value stream.
4. Other Kaizen/Lean tools. All of the traditional Lean tools such as standardized work, one piece flow cells, Kanban/pull, visual controls, quick changeover/single minute exchange of die (SMED), 5S, total productive maintenance, and others can help improve a supply chain.

The downfall of a *Kaizen Event* is when these four tools are not implemented in unison.

Philosophy

The Kaizen strategy is the single most important concept in Japanese management. It is the key to Japanese competitive success. Because of Japan's success, the Kaizen philosophy has been implemented in organizations around the world as a way to improve production values while also improving employee morale and safety. The Kaizen philosophy may be applied to any workplace scenario due to its simple nature. However, we are aware that every organization has specific needs.

Kaizen provides small improvements and a change for the better. It must be accompanied by a change of method. The Kaizen concept stimulates productivity improvement as an ongoing process in any company. It is a practice-oriented strategy which leads to creation of culture of improvement. It is more a way of life or at least a cultural approach to quality improvement. The implementation of philosophy of Kaizen can be achieved through the involvement of employees to effect improvements.

Kaizen can be implemented in any type of industry to improve every aspect of the business process in a step-by-step approach, while gradually developing employee skills through training and increased involvement. The principles are:

• Human resources are the most important company asset.
• The process must evolve by gradual improvement rather than radical changes.
• Improvement must be based on evaluation of process performance.

By practicing Kaizen culture, managers demonstrate commitment to quality. Also, the workers with adequate support from managers become a major source of improvement.

Kaizen method is genius in its simplicity, but its repercussions are far reaching. These can be in the areas, internally or externally, of productivity, quality, cost, delivery, safety, and morale of employees.

These far-reaching repercussions are a product of our understanding of the six steps of the Kaizen philosophy. The six steps are as follows:

Step 1: Standardize – the first thing you will need to do is come up with a process for what you are trying to do. A great example would be, if you worked on a home clean up team, what steps would you take to complete the job from start to finish? You have to remember, this process needs to be repeatable as well as organized.

Step 2: Measure – next, you need to be able to measure your results. Back to the house cleaning job, measure how long it takes you now compared to last time. You could also measure completion time, customer satisfaction, and so on.

Step 3: Compare – now you need to go back and measure your results against your requirements. This step will help you figure out if your method is working, or lacking something crucial. Find out if your method is saving you time, and accomplishing the goal that you set out to complete.

Step 4: Innovate – once you are done with comparing, start looking at other ways to get things done –even if you are content with the first results. The odds are, the first way we pick to get things done is not always going to be the best. The important thing to remember about this step is it really helps you explore your options and find smarter, quicker, and more efficient routes to get things done.

Step 5: Standardize – yes, now you must go back and create more repeatable processes for the things you are trying to get accomplished. It is important to keep remembering that these need to be measurable, and different from the first way you worked before.

Step 6: Repeat – go back to step one and start the entire process all over again.

It might seem like a tiring process at first, but it will get you results. It is a mindset that will stick with you before long, and you will start constantly looking for new and inventive ways to improve. The first couple times you try to adopt the Kaizen philosophy you might struggle because we tend to avoid change. You should stick with it, though, to receive the results that you deserve.

Structure

The approach to Kaizen in supply chain via the total flow management system is one that includes the entire supply chain of a given company. The starting point for the design is the point where you are located in the supply chain. Maybe your organization is a manufacturing facility or a product-distribution facility. By applying the model, you will be creating your internal pull-flow system and also considering how you can expand this model, both downstream of your supply chain and upstream.

Let's take the different supply chain flows from the perspective of a single manufacturing plant. The delivery of raw materials and components from suppliers to the plant are regular, high-frequency transport loops. Manufacturing is pulled from the retail customer on the basis of continuous real demand requirements. Similarly, forecasts are also sent from retail customers, to be used for capacity-planning purpose only.

The main target is the reduction of the total lead time in the supply chain. The measure of lead time is the inventory coverage across the entire supply chain. It is called 'lead time' and not 'coverage' because the inventory coverage is usually a good estimate of the time it takes one individual product unit to cross the chain.

Reducing lead time also eliminates the waste of waiting and really means creating a material flow. Rigorous systems, processes, and standards are required to create and maintain this flow and to ensure the following:

1. Reduced cost
2. Reduced working capital
3. Increased productivity
4. Improved quality
5. Higher level of customer service and satisfaction

This is achieved by creating a flow across the entire supply chain, starting with customer consumption, that is, production can be driven by real orders or inventory – replenishment orders. Forecasts will no longer be used for creating production or distribution orders; rather, they will be used only for capacity management.

At the same time, the system works to change the company culture to one that is based on the Kaizen spirit of improvement every day, everywhere, and by everybody.

Application

The global business environment for manufacturers has never been more competitive. As the adage goes, a company's performance relative to its rivals is either getting better or getting worse – it never stays the same. However, while manufacturing executives are aware that they need to constantly improve their firm's processes, actually quantifying that improvement is difficult, and figuring out a way to systematically improve company performance on a continuous basis is even more so.

In the late 1980s, several multi-national manufacturing corporations trying to identify a method to continuously improve company processes came up with the 'Kaizen Event.' A regularly scheduled gathering of employees from all areas of a firm, Kaizen Events are designed to focus that collective experience on any number of individual challenges.

Kaizen Events can be powerful tools to make improvement a continuous and structured effort. What follows is a brief introduction to Kaizen Events and how and when incorporated the concept improves our ongoing operations. We hope you'll find it a helpful introduction to implementing Kaizen Events that can be easily tailored to your business.

Kaizen is a Japanese term meaning 'improvement' or 'improving one's self for the benefit of the whole'. The concept grew out of a wider movement to tackle the critical but elusive task of continuously improving manufacturing processes – this as opposed to just doing things as they've always been done and only introducing occasional improvements piecemeal without an overarching plan. But how do you create a set of protocols that allow you to apply an actionable framework to that improvement? How do you not only make it efficient but enforce a schedule on it and make it reproducible?

We all remember that Motorola was the first to spearhead the effort to systematically address these challenges with the so-called 'Six Sigma' approach. The term is borrowed from manufacturing – a 'sigma rating' indicates the percentage of products produced that are free from defects. A 'six sigma' process is one in which more than 99.99% of products are defect-free.

Kaizen Events are part of this approach to reduce inefficiencies and increase the quality not only of products but also of the processes that create them. Hypothetically, the concepts behind Kaizen Events are simple and are as follows:

- During a period of 3–5 days, employees from a cross-section of departments meet in one place to discuss the process at hand. The participants are all stakeholders in that process, and are usually derived from all areas of the company, from management to administration. The idea is to bring the greatest breadth and depth of knowledge and experience into the discussion.
- The group observes the process. This can either be in the form of a demonstration or, if it's more practical, through the creation of a flowchart or a value stream map of the steps involved.
- Once the participants understand the process, they make suggestions to improve it.
- Finally, the group discusses options, during which suggestions are either implemented or discarded, until all participants can get behind the new approach.

The primary traits of Kaizen Events are their efficiency and their focus. They gather the decision makers and the people actually involved in the process in one place at one time. A particular strength of Kaizen Events is that they get everyone's buy-in so that thoughtful, effective solutions can be implemented quickly. Companies can make rapid improvements, particularly with a process that isn't running particularly efficiently.

Typically, the plant manager will spearhead a Kaizen Event, along with a team leader. Also included will be 4–5 employees from all departments to provide a diverse and unbiased observation group. The team assembles in the area where the process to be evaluated takes place, such as the manufacturing process floor. However, these events don't just consider manufacturing processes. They can extend to all aspects of the company, including shipping and receiving, inventory management, engineering, and sales.

The team observes the full process. On the manufacturing side, Kaizen Events are most often concentrated on safety and efficiency. Some things that team members might consider:

- Do they notice something unusual that the operator who works in that area every day might have long since gotten used to?
- Is the operator performing tasks that appear to be unsafe, and could they be done in a safer way?
- Is the movement of the operator efficient and ergonomic, i.e. is there too much bending and lifting involved?
- Are the parts or tools needed for the process inefficiently located?

After observing the process, the team meets to discuss each group member's observations and decide on any action items that could be implemented. The current process is documented, issues or problems are defined, and possible changes are discussed. Suggestions may encompass changes in a work area to improve ergonomics, safety, efficiency, work flow, etc. Any approved changes are implemented, and a follow up of the process is scheduled to evaluate the results.

Although Kaizen Events have proven their ability to increase efficiency, boost productivity, and provide a program that enables continuous improvement of production processes, many companies are still reluctant to implement them. One primary reason is the perception that such events take employees away from their 'primary functions' for up to five days at a time. While this concern is understandable, we've found it to be a short-sighted view. In fact, in our experience, proper application of Kaizen Events has led to better performance in employees' 'primary functions', allowing them to place more focus on quality rather than the process. The events help employees identify ways to spend the majority of time in their primary roles more efficiently, rather than having to frequently 'put out fires' and attempt to manage universal problems with quick fixes over and over again.

Another potential drawback is that companies implement only part of the program or event. Rather than committing a meaningful number of people for a meaningful period of time, some firms will instead commit a couple of people for an insufficient amount of time. The result is fewer suggestions for improvement, and a perception on the part of employees that decision makers view the effort as unimportant.

Kaizen Events are not a cure-all. If a recurring problem requires evaluating sets of data over an extended period of time – statistical analysis or variations in long-term experimental results – a carefully selected team of experts that meets regularly will likely be a better choice than a one-time meeting of disparate individuals. Kaizen Events are much better suited to recurring methods and processes.

Kaizen Events must be championed by management and enjoy the full participation of a variety of employees. During the course of the event, employees on Kaizen Event teams must:

1. Undergo a brief training period that will allow them to grasp the process more fully
2. Go into the event with precisely defined goals, outlined in steps 3–5
3. Acquire a full understanding of the current approach to the process
4. Be encouraged to think and entertain ideas or concepts that might go against the 'grain' of normal activity
5. Develop a plan to follow up on improvements and assess their effectiveness

Of all the steps listed above, number 4 is perhaps the most critical and the toughest to establish. Employees must believe that any ideas they may come up with to address problems are important and valued. They must also be assured that any improvements they suggest won't put them or other employees out of a job. Any successes should be highlighted and shared within the company so that everyone can appreciate and understand the value of Kaizen Events.

Most importantly, effective Kaizen Events require and foster respect. They show that each area of a company is no longer considered an independent silo or entity, that each department has something important to contribute, that each person in every department is an important part of the team, and that each individual is willing and able to improve the experience of everyone else who works there.

5

THE 5S

What is 5S?

5S is a workplace organization method that uses a list of five Japanese words: *seiri, seiton, seisō, seiketsu,* and *shitsuke.* These have been translated as 'Sort', 'Set In order', 'Shine', 'Standardize', and 'Sustain'. The list describes how to organize a work space for efficiency and effectiveness by identifying and storing the items used, maintaining the area and items, and sustaining the new order. The decision-making process usually comes from a dialogue about standardization, which builds understanding among employees of how they should do the work.

Other than a specific stand-alone methodology, 5S is frequently viewed as an element of a broader construct known as *visual control, visual workplace,* or *visual factory.* Under those similar terminologies, Western companies were applying underlying concepts of 5S before publication, in English, of the formal 5S methodology.

5S was developed in Japan and was identified as one of the techniques that enabled just-in-time manufacturing. A major framework for understanding and applying 5S to business environments has arisen – providing a structure to improve programs with a series of identifiable steps, each building on its predecessor.

In simple terms, the five S methodology helps a workplace remove items that are no longer needed (sort), organize the items to optimize efficiency and flow (straighten), clean the area in order to more easily identify problems (shine), implement color coding and labels to stay consistent with other areas (standardize), and develop behaviors that keep the workplace organized over the long term (sustain).

Definitions

Following are the definitions and breakdown of each 'S':

1. **Sort (*seiri*)** – distinguishing between necessary and unnecessary things, and getting rid of what you do not need.

   - Remove items not used in the area – outdated materials, broken equipment, redundant equipment, files on the computer, measurements which you no longer use.
   - Ask staff to tag all items which they don't think are needed – this improves understanding about need and use.
   - Classify all equipment and materials by frequency of use to help decide if it should be removed – place '**Red Tag**' on items to be removed.
   - Establish a 'holding area' for items that are difficult to classify – hold item for allotted period to enable others not on the 5S team to review.

2. **Straighten (*seiton*)** – the practice of orderly storage so the right item can be picked efficiently (without waste) at the right time, easy to access for everyone. A place for everything and everything in its place.

   - Identify and allocate a place for all the materials needed for your work.
   - Assign fixed places and fixed quantity.
   - Make it compact.
   - Place heavy objects at a height where they are easy to pick from.
   - Decide how things should be put away, and obey those rules.

3. **Shine (*seisō*)** – creating a clean worksite without garbage, dirt, and dust, so problems can be more easily identified (leaks, spills, excess, damage, etc.)

   • Identify root causes of dirtiness, and correct processes.
   • Perform only one work activity on a workspace at any given time.
   • Keep tools and equipment clean and in top condition, ready for use at any time.
   • Ensure cleanliness is followed as part of a daily activity – at least 5 minutes per day.
   • Use charts with signatures/initials to show that the action or review has taken place.
   • Ensure proper lighting – it can be hard to see dirt and dust.

4. **Standardize (*seiketsu*)** – setting up standards for a neat, clean workplace.

   • Standardize best practices through 'visual management'.
   • Make abnormalities visible to management.
   • Keep areas consistent with one another.
   • Standards make it easy to move workers into different areas.
   • Create a process to maintain the standard, defining roles and responsibilities.
   • Make it easy for everyone to identify the state of normal or abnormal conditions – place photos on the walls to provide a visual reminder.

5. **Sustain (*shitsuke*)** – implementing behaviors and habits to maintain the established standards over the long term, and making the workplace organization the key to managing the process for success. This is the toughest phase to sustain – many fall short of this goal.

   • Establish and maintain responsibilities – requires leader's commitment to follow through.
   • Ensure everyone sticks to the rules and makes it a habit.
   • Engage everyone in developing good habits and buy-in.
   • Hold regular audits and reviews.
   • Get to root cause of issues.
   • Aim for higher 5S levels – continuous improvement.

Effective 5S components

While the concepts are easy to understand, most companies have not implemented them. Implementation of 5S has many benefits: higher quality, lower costs, reliable deliveries, and improved safety, to name a few. These benefits are clearly relevant to any manufacturer, and they are not had simply by eliminating toolboxes and cleaning up. The intent of 5S is to have only what you need available in the workplace, a designated place for everything, a standard way of doing things, and the discipline to maintain it.

The components of 5S create a superior working environment. They give the employee an opportunity to provide creative input regarding how the workplace should be organized and laid out and how standard work should be done. Employees will be able to find things easily, every time. The workplace will be cleaner and safer. Jobs will be simpler and more satisfying with many obstacles and frustrations removed.

The 5S philosophy

5S is one of the first tools that can be applied in a company that is starting down the path of the continuous improvement culture. A 5S implementation helps to define the first rules to eliminate waste and maintain an efficient, safe, and clean work environment. The 5S methodology is easy for everyone to start using. It doesn't require any technical analysis, and can be implemented globally in all types of companies, ranging from manufacturing plants to offices, small businesses to large multi-national organizations – and in both private and public sectors. Its simplicity, practical applicability, and visual nature make it an engaging aid for operators, directors, and customers alike.

5S is the perfect tool to identify the first improvement projects in your company to eliminate. Although sometimes viewed as a housekeeping technique, it is actually an innovative management system that helps people think Lean, paving the way for the adoption of Lean. Understanding the 5S methodology is one of the foundations of Lean principles, and can be extremely beneficial for organizations of all kinds.

And here's the best part: implementing 5S is a breeze! With this logical, step-by-step guide, you'll learn what the big deal about 5S is, how to devise an action plan for 5S implementation, and how best to wield this powerful tool for improved productivity, elimination of wasteful processes, and all-round development!

6

THE 5 WHYS

The 5 Whys is a probing technique used to explore the cause-and-effect relationships underlying a particular problem. The primary goal of the technique is to determine the root cause of a defect by repeating the question 'Why?'. Each answer forms the basis of the next question. The '5' in the name derives from an anecdotal observation on the number of iterations needed to resolve the problem.

Not all problems have a single root cause. If one wishes to uncover multiple root causes, the method must be repeated, asking a different sequence of questions each time.

The method provides no hard and fast rules about what lines of questions to explore, or how long to continue the search for additional root causes. Thus, even when the method is closely followed, the outcome still depends upon the knowledge and persistence of the people involved.

While the 5 Whys is a powerful tool for engineers or technically savvy individuals to help get to the true causes of problems, it has been criticized as being too basic a tool to analyze root causes to the depth that is needed to ensure that they are fixed. Reasons for this criticism include:

- Tendency for investigators to stop at symptoms rather than going on to lower-level root causes
- Inability to go beyond the investigator's current knowledge – the investigator cannot find causes that they do not already know
- Lack of support to help the investigator ask the right 'why' questions
- Results are not repeatable – different people using 5 Whys come up with different causes for the same problem
- Tendency to isolate a single root cause, whereas each question could elicit many different root causes

These can be significant problems when the method is applied through deduction only. To avoid these issues, it is recommended that the answer to the current 'why' question is verified before proceeding to the next question.

For these reasons, I am a proponent of the *Five Flows* of the supply chain. The supply chain is the management of flows – product, financial, information, value, and risk. Each one shall be discussed in detail below.

Product flow

Product flow includes movement of goods from supplier to consumer, as well as dealing with customer service needs such as input materials or consumables or services like housekeeping. Product flow also involves returns/rejections – reverse logistics.

In a typical industry situation, there will be a supplier, manufacturer, distributor, wholesaler, retailer, and consumer. The consumer may even be an internal customer in the same organization. For example, in a manufacturing environment the raw materials warehouse is the customer of the receiving department, manufacturing is the customer of the raw material warehouse department, etc. Flow in such a company is from one process department to the other, in a supplier-consumer (internal) relationship. Acquisition is taking place at each stage from the previous stage along the entire flow in the supply chain.

In the supply chain the goods and services generally flow downstream (forward) from the source or point of origin to consumer or point of consumption. There is also a backward (or upstream) flow of materials, mainly associated with product returns.

Financial flow

The financial and economic aspect of supply chain management shall be considered from two viewpoints: first, from the cost and investment perspective and, second, based upon the flow of funds. The optimization of total supply chain cost contributes directly (and often very significantly) to overall profitability. Similarly, optimization of supply chain investment contributes to the optimization of return on the capital employed in a company. In a supply chain, from the ultimate consumer of the product back down through the chain there will be flow of funds. Revenues flow from the final consumer, who is usually the only source of 'real' money in a supply chain, back through the other links in the chain (typically retailers, distributors, processors, and suppliers).

In any organization, the supply chain has both accounts payable and accounts receivable activities and includes payment schedules, credit, and additional financial arrangements. Funds flow in opposite directions: receivables (funds inflow) and payables (funds outflow). The working capital cycle also provides a useful representation of financial flows in a supply chain. Great opportunities and challenges therefore lie ahead in managing financial flows in supply chains. The integrated management of this flow is a key to supply chain management activity, and one which has a direct impact on the cash flow position and profitability of the company.

Information flow

Supply chain management involves a great deal of diverse information – bills of materials, product data, big data, descriptions and pricing, inventory levels, customer and order information, delivery scheduling, supplier and distributor information, delivery status, commercial documents, title of goods, current cash flow and financial information, etc. This requires a lot of communication, collaboration, and coordination with suppliers, transportation vendors, subcontractors, and other parties. Information flows in the supply chain are multidirectional. Faster and better information flow enhances supply chain effectiveness and information technology has greatly transformed the performance.

Value flow

A supply chain has a series of value-creating processes which extend over the entire chain in order to provide added value to the end consumer. At each stage there are physical flows relating to production and distribution which lead to addition of value to the products or services. Even a retailer who doesn't transform or alter the product provides value-added services like making the product available at a convenient place in small lots.

These can be referred to as value chains because as the product moves from one point to another, it gains value. A value chain is a series of interconnected activities which are required to bring a product or service from conception, through the different phases of production (involving a combination of physical transformation and the input of various product services), delivery to final customers, and final disposal after use. Thus value chain and supply chain are complementing and supplementing each other. In practice, supply chains with value flow are more complex, involving more than one chain, and these channels can have more than one originating supply point and final point of consumption.

In the supply chain at each such activity there are costs, revenues, and asset values allocated. Either through controlling cost drivers better than before or better than competitors or by reconfiguring the value chain, sustainable competitive advantage is achieved.

Risk flow

Risks in supply chain are due to various uncertain elements covered under demand, supply, price, lead time, etc. Supply chain risk is a potential occurrence of an incident or failure to seize opportunities of supplying the customer in which its outcomes result in financial loss for the whole supply chain. Risks therefore can appear as any kind of disruptions, price volatility, and poor perceived quality of the product or service, process/ internal quality failures, deficiency of physical infrastructure, natural disaster, or any event damaging the reputation of the firm. Risk factors also include cash flow constraints, inventory financing, and delayed cash payment. Risks can be external or internal and move either way with product or financial or information or value flow.

External risks can be driven by events either upstream or downstream in the supply chain:

- Demand risks – related to unpredictable or misunderstood customer or end-customer demand
- Supply risks – related to any disturbances to the flow of product within your supply chain
- Environment risks – originate from shocks outside the supply chain
- Business risks – related to factors such as suppliers' financial or management stability
- Physical risks – related to the condition of a supplier's physical facilities

Internal risks are driven by events within company control:

- Manufacturing risks – caused by disruptions of internal operations or processes
- Business risks – caused by changes in key personnel, management, reporting structures, or business processes
- Planning and control risks – caused by inadequate assessment and planning, and ineffective management
- Mitigation and contingency risks – caused by not putting in place contingencies

The containment or mitigation of both internal and external risks have been magnified and are increasing in the global economy, especially as new underdeveloped economies are emerging in various and far-flung parts of the world.

Successful supply chain management integrates the five flow processes from end user through original suppliers, manufacturer, and third-party logistics partners in a supply chain. Integration is a critical achievement factor in a dynamic market environment and is a must for enhancing value in the system. For effective performance of the supply chain, a precondition is sharing and the utilization of resources, assets, facilities, and processes. Sharing of information, knowledge, and systems between different layers in the chain is vital for the success of each chain in improving lead times, process execution efficiencies and costs, quality of the process, inventory costs, and information transfer in a supply chain. Integration of these flows leads to better collaboration for coordinated production, scheduling, collaborative product development, collaborative demand, and logistic planning. With increased information transparency and relevant operational knowledge and data exchange, integrated supply chain partners can be more responsive to volatile demands resulting from frequent changes in competition, technology, regulations, etc. Integration is required not only for economic benefits but also for compliances in terms of social and community, diversity, environment, ethics, financial responsibility, human rights, safety, organizational policies, industry code of conduct, and various national and international laws, regulations, standards, and issues.

Part 2

DIGITALIZATION OF SUPPLY CHAIN PROCUREMENT

Procurement refers to all of the tasks involved in obtaining the optimal product from the optimal vendor, on optimal terms. Procurement involves processes that occur before a purchase is made, as it is made, and after the actual transaction has been completed.

Pre-purchase procurement involves:

- Defining your organization's needs
- Conducting research on solutions offered by potential suppliers
- Determining which of your options poses the best opportunity for success

Procurement *during* a purchase involves:

- Negotiating terms with your chosen supplier
- Creating a purchase order
- Fulfilling your end of the agreement

Finally, procurement on the other side of the purchase will have your company engaging with your suppliers repeatedly and more intensively over time, both for purchasing and for other reasons.

For example, you might inquire as to whether a supplier offers related products or services that might allow you to get even more value out of the original purchase.

Procurement focuses on the context behind the business you do with your vendors, allowing you to move forward in the most mutually beneficial way possible.

1

THE REINVENTION OF PROCUREMENT

In today's demand-driven manufacturing and supply chain world, your company faces growing challenges around market volatility, long lead times, and forecasting errors. Your inventory management decisions can make or break your firm's financial bottom line. Lean procurement principles' solutions let your company meet these daily challenges and protect your bottom line every day.

Companies expect their procurement and supply chain organizations to provide purchased materials and assemblies on time, all the time, to meet their customer demands. Faced with these poor market forecasts, buyers often over buy requirements. This creates excess inventories. Purchasing organizations cannot afford long material lead times. And if suppliers cannot deliver consistently on time, they will be replaced. Although better than traditional procurement practices, today's supply chain replenishment processes are not optimized, collaborative, or effective.

Today, the buyer's responsibilities have changed dramatically. Beyond simply finding the right materials and services at the best price, buyers play a critical part. 'The automation of procurement execution as part of pull-based replenishment of direct materials is driving true process collaboration between manufacturers and suppliers. With the aid of technology companies can expect to streamline buyer productivity, eliminate non-value-added activities, reduce direct material inventory across the supply chain, and improve the supply network's capability to meet customer demand. Your supply chain will determine if your company will survive and thrive in today's competitive procurement marketplace.

A world and context evolving

In order to understand the future of procurement, it is necessary for a brief review of its history and evolution. In the past, procurement was a back-office function tied to processing transactions as opposed to an integral part of the supply chain. The choice of suppliers and negotiations with suppliers was unsystematic and not very demanding.

By the 1990s this began to change due to the introduction of strategic sourcing. Since that time, this simple yet influential discipline has delivered huge savings within numerous companies and procurement has gained a 'seat' at the supply chain table.

There are many questions to be asked using strategic sourcing, but a number come to mind:

1. How can a company safeguard itself against devastating supply chain interruptions?
2. How does a company cope with the changing global economics and the emerging markets?
3. What are the capabilities a company will require to maintain a profitable international business?
4. How will an organization sustain its business in the face of protectionist demands?

These are the questions that every procurement manager should be constantly grappling with in order to withstand and embrace disruptions from natural disasters, changing technologies, digitalization of the supply chain, and geo-political issues.

What this means is simply this: *the drivers of past success will not engineer future success.*

In the past, procurement was seen through the eyes of manufacturing. However, by 1994, per the US GDP services were at 55%. Clearly, the type of procurement has changed and companies need to catch up. A service-oriented company requires procurement to develop new strategies and competencies. Today a company must forge a partnership with its supplier/suppliers to explore ways of working together for mutual benefit. The traditional methods of procurement in a manufacturing environment fails to be an effective weapon in this new age of suppliers of services whose value is derived from intangible assets.

Procurement departments of the new 21st-century supply chain require new guidelines, policies, and processes to gain value from different sourcing circumstances – legal, marketing, advertising, research, design, and engineering. In the past, these categories were off limits to procurement but this is no longer true in this new age of procurement.

To borrow a phrase from Aldous Huxley, 'it's a brave new world.' Service procurement is quite different from sourcing materials in the following ways. Firstly, economies of scale do not reduce unit costs in the same way as a manufacturing company. Secondly, the profit drivers are distinct from those of manufacturing. Additionally, the primary asset of service suppliers is people. Procurement needs to think differently about control, risk, and value with suppliers whose sole purpose is to sell services.

Procurement models

Traditional	New
Cost reduction	Solving issues
Competitive pressure	Collaboration with suppliers
Shareholder focus	Trusted advisor
Transactions	Relationships
Analytics	Soft skills

With any new implementation of methodologies it should be accompanied by a new set of metrics or key performance indicators (KPIs) in order to measure the efficiency and effectiveness of the new method. One such new metric is 'revenue-at-risk'. This is a more complex calculation but one that is more meaningful as it measures external expenses linked to the customer revenue stream. It is another metric that might seem questionable as to how to measure, but it will tell the story about how well the idea of collaboration is being used. Procurement should partner with marketing and product design to select a suitable supplier for packaging material. The three departments found such a supplier, the cost being higher, but with an expanded market, increased revenue, and higher margins, it paid off in the long term.

Along with new metrics, there must be new competencies for the employees in procurement, especially since most of the former work is being outsourced – PO processing and market analysis. Procurement must develop competencies that are more difficult to replace with software or by outsourcing. There are three competencies that procurement needs to enhance. They are the following:

1. Business acumen: analytical skills to calculate total cost of ownership are valuable. But the new procurement must think like a business owner – understand the business models of suppliers and how they make money.
2. Strategy development: a long-term plan that speaks to important choices and explains why difficult choices must be made.
3. Soft skills: an increasing interest in building skills for a more strategic approach to negotiate based on honorable persuasion and joint problem solving. Some of the soft skills include relationship building, conflict management, change management, and leadership.

Different industries encounter different procurement issues with the pressure to bring processes into the 21st century, along with new technological innovations. However, any procurement department or organization that wishes to enhance its financial value to its firm must evolve and mature.

2

THE TRANSFORMATION OF PROCUREMENT INTO A GLOBAL FORCE

Tactical versus strategic!

While it is fair to call the last decade transformational for procurement as a function, most procurement organizations are learning to break away from back-office viewpoints and are moving to the corporate forefront. Slowly but surely, it's becoming more widely recognized that procurement delivers a unique strategic advantage and value to our respective companies.

While this transformation is happening at a functional level, behind the curtains most procurement organizations are still busy addressing what is commonly considered to be tactical work: responding to contract requests, managing supplier communications, running RFPs, and preparing supplier scorecards. While category management has been adopted as a principle, when it comes to practice, most organizations continue to struggle with achieving or sustaining it along with a flurry of other tactical responsibilities.

This chapter discusses the essential components that allow procurement departments to shift from a tactical mindset to strategic management. We'll examine topics such as resource limitations, skills gaps, training, and knowledge management, as well as procurement's overall reputation.

Let's take a look at how we think about tactical and strategic as procurement concepts, as well as what qualifies as tactical work versus what qualifies as strategic work. Are the following activities tactical or strategic activities?

- Securing a global supply base that meets the organization's cost targets to manufacture a highly efficient vehicle that needs to be a cost leader in its respective markets.
- Developing new call-center capabilities in a low-cost South American country that meets the localization and customer service needs of your organization and grows a South American presence.
- Meeting with your top IT-services suppliers and brainstorming on how they can implement a variable fee structure to support your organization's unpredictable demand patterns.
- When renewing your next outsourcing contract, embedding some risk-reward incentive to ensure suppliers are vested in the success and outcomes of initiatives that are a top-3 priority for your company.

What is your role in the procurement process? Are the methods used by your procurement department earning the most value for the company? Are you confident that there isn't a more effective way for your organization to purchase the goods and services it needs?

With companies focusing more and more on optimizing their spend, it has become essential for procurement to find ways to reduce waste and save more money. Procurement is becoming increasingly more involved in the overall objectives of the company.

Therefore, for a company to be successful, it requires procurement to follow industry best practices for getting the greatest value in what it buys. The question that should be asked is, 'what is the most effective way for my organization to obtain the goods and services it needs to function properly?'.

Perhaps, the best manner to illustrate the new digital age for supply chain would be a case study. Since this is an ongoing client I am unable to divulge their name. However, the case study should pinpoint the need to digitalize the supply chain of many companies. I will break the project down into the following: the background, the approach, and then, results.

Background:

Global manufacturer of highly technical machine parts for a variety of industries. Despite being an established leader in their field, their financial position and sales revenue had been eroded by historically low market prices. To breach the disparity, our client sought to dramatically reduce third-party spend expenditures. From a procurement perspective the task was complicated by the fact that the client's three subsidiaries have operated quite independently of each other. As a result, there was a disjointed supplier base and little, if any, consistency across business units. The procurement approach was predominantly transactional. There was little focus on developing strategic long-term relationships with suppliers and limited cooperation between purchasing, engineering, and quality functions. To address these issues and ensure the savings were achievable and sustainable, it became necessary to transform the procurement function, establish a global supply chain management organization, and retrain the procurement staff.

Approach:

We began with conducting a six-week audit assessment across all business units. This identified targeted savings of $21 million across 12 direct material categories and $225 million in spend. Two successive sourcing audits were designed, with $15 million targeted savings in each wave.

Direct materials, comprising the largest spend categories, were the primary focus. These are more complex to source, because they directly impact the specification, production, and performance of the client's end products. As a result, close cooperation between procurement, engineering, and quality functions was critical to the success of the program – but the fragmented nature of the existing procurement approach meant this would require a whole new way of working. We addressed this by setting up multi-site teams, which brought together different parts of the business. These teams were responsible for jointly reviewing product specifications, aligning them across business units, and choosing suppliers that offered the best strategic value. Over 10,000 technical drawings were validated and categorized.

To ensure sustainable change, a new global supply chain organization was put into action. This included selecting the best people within the organization and upgrading their skill levels through a comprehensive training program.

Results:

At present, the new project has succeeded in achieving our client's objectives. The first audit has delivered $14 million of signed-off savings, with the second audit underway. Importantly, the savings have translated to the bottom line, with P&L savings on target. The program has also delivered many ongoing benefits. The process of bringing procurement staff from each business unit together has created an integrated procurement approach across the company with a much more strategic, long-term focus. It also succeeded in bringing procurement together with other key stakeholders in the supply chain. This forged work in a collaborative way to find solutions rather than working in silos. This process has allowed local issues to be understood and addressed in the context of wider business needs, and helped build credibility for procurement within the business.

Due to the complexity and inter-dependencies of these trends and the diversity of growing new markets, it's difficult to assess the impact on procurement but leading procurement managers foresee major changes in a couple of focal areas within the next decade: global sourcing, risk management, and supplier relationships. Future professional procurement and supply chain management will look different from now and will require strong leadership and change management by CPOs (Chief Procurement Officers) to earn a seat at the table and transform procurement to a partner of choice.

3

PROCUREMENT AND DIGITALIZATION

Some call it 'digitalization', some call it 'smart manufacturing', and others call it 'the next industrial revolution'. Whatever term you use, a combination of new technologies – from big data analytics to 3D printing to machine learning – is revolutionizing companies' operational and administrative processes and creating innovative digital products and services.

Reflecting the effects of cutting-edge technologies and data management on strategic and operational procurement, the idea of 'Procurement 4.0' has recently been coined. What does Procurement 4.0 entail? Will it be the strategic compass for chief procurement officers (CPOs) in the future? There are many opinions, and every company will ultimately require its own strategy as it pursues both the challenges and the opportunities that come with advanced procurement.

In industries across the board, however, companies need to consider the way digital innovation will disrupt not only the way their organizations work today but the entire spectrum of procurement – suppliers, customers, and internal process partners. In this chapter I will discuss the framework for adapting to the organizational changes that a 21st-century approach to procurement will require.

This new framework will start with six areas. Each will be discussed below.

New procurement value proposition: chief procurement officers need to rethink the value added by procurement within the company. With the new opportunities provided by digitalization and big data, traditional organizational boundaries between research and development, manufacturing, procurement, and, in some cases, the entire supply chain will become increasingly blurred.

The procurement division, as the primary owner of the supplier interface, can keep its distinctive value proposition within the company by seizing some of these new opportunities. It can create new business models for itself and move from being a cost center to a profit center. This is possible because procurement possesses strategic know-how about suppliers and their markets and a deep expertise about the goods and services that are procured, as well as the alternatives on offer, including emerging innovations. All of this knowledge represents an asset that is gaining tremendous value in today's market.

Digital category and service procurement: new technologies will lead to new business needs, which will be reflected in new requirements for the procurement department. One of these requirements will be capturing, analyzing, and acting on real-time data, an activity at the heart of Procurement 4.0. Increasingly, data will be transmitted using sensors, analyzed in real time, and all the while being made available in real time to supply chain partners. People, objects, and systems will be increasingly connected through data communications, transforming value chains into larger 'value networks' – *sets of connections between organizations and individuals interacting with each other to benefit the entire group.* For procurement, this will mean that certain items, such as intelligent bar codes, RFIDs, and associated software, will be sourced much more frequently than before. Certain categories of items such as electronics will grow, while others may shrink and even disappear.

Not only will companies change what they buy as they incorporate Procurement 4.0, but importantly, they will also change the ways in which they buy. The purchasing of services will increase dramatically, for example, leading to a need for many new and different contracting approaches to ensure that companies receive the best value for their money. In addition, there will be many intellectual property implications around ownership of the data collected by the software when the end products are sold and in use. Who owns the rights to this data?

Digital supply chain and supplier management: it has been a manufacturing dream for ages, the ability to integrate all of the data from customers, distributors, production, and suppliers in real time to optimize supply chain performance. It has become clear that this dream will not be realized by big ERP-centered providers. Instead, a host of agile specialized providers such as Kinaxis and Elementum will integrate ERP, manufacturing execution systems, and manufacturing and logistics data from all the partners in a given value chain. As this Procurement 4.0 data integration takes place, procurement will play an integral role in getting suppliers on board and optimizing the end-to-end supply chain.

Data integration will substantially change supplier management as well. Companies will be able to employ big data analytics, looking at enormous quantities of customer, financial, and external data – from the weather all the way to credit ratings – to predict changes in risk ratings. They will have the additional option of feeding changes in credit ratings automatically into the supplier risk management system.

Innovative procurement data utilization: data analytics is probably the most important facilitator for Procurement 4.0. Smart technologies and algorithms allow very large volumes of data from many heterogeneous sources to be aggregated, processed, and analyzed. The resulting analyses can be used to understand suppliers, internal and external markets, and customers, and look into machine and product failures. They can enable employers to make better and more informed decisions. These will be the drivers of the 'new' procurement departments.

Analyzing data and using it cleverly is one of the key success factors for companies that want to make the most of Procurement 4.0. It will be procurement's responsibility to ensure that all of the opportunities offered to the company through the analysis of big data are maximized, working with suppliers to allow both company and supplier to benefit from the resultant improvements in supply chain efficiency.

Digital processes and tools: digital technologies will help procurement increase collaboration, analytics, and engagement using a spectrum of tools along the entire procurement value chain, from planning and sourcing to contract negotiations, order delivery, payment, and supplier management. These technologies vary greatly in their impact and current technological maturity. Companies will need to look carefully at both conditions as they lay out an IT architecture strategy that will specify the processes they want to support and the tools they want to use, based on a valued procurement road map. Whatever the strategy, an organization must have digital procurement processes included with digital requests for quotations, supplier financial analysis, procurement risk analysis, e-signatures and verification, and digital procurement network collaboration.

Note that investing in new digital tools is a means to an end, not the end itself. Ideally, this investment will lead to digitally automated processes, even beyond the transactional purchase-to-pay, with only limited manual support required. Such digital tools and processes will additionally support business process outsourcing and shared-services centers, further boosting efficiency. Ultimately, however, the benefits will arise not simply from reducing costs but also from freeing up highly qualified procurement resources from mundane, repetitive tasks so they can focus on delivering value to the business.

Organization and capabilities: it is clear that the first five elements of the framework pose a tremendous change to the way of working for procurement that they require a fundamental regrouping regarding organization and capabilities, both of which will need to be reshaped over time. Companies will need to create new job profiles for buyers of new categories of items, contract experts on intellectual property, or data scientists for data maintenance, analysis, and mining. To locate this talent, new sources must be unlocked with the help of procurement cooperation partners such as university partnership programs and research centers, along with social networks, social media, and top-performing employees rehired after a few years' absence. The largest companies should consider establishing their own procurement academies to conduct webinars, cross-functional training, and supplier workshops. Only if procurement personnel are digitally capable can a company fully benefit from the opportunities provided through digitalization.

In addition, digitalization will increase globalization and speed up communications in an ever more closely connected world. Whereas it was once enough to have knowledge about certain supply markets such as China and Eastern Europe, Procurement 4.0 will require an organization that is truly global. For example, having the core of the procurement organization housed at headquarters might have worked in the past, but looking ahead, more and more buyers may need to be located in the most competitive supply markets for each category.

Even though these six areas of new processes are near established within companies many CPOs are asking other questions that require immediate answers to ensure competitive advantage.

1. Which of the new digital solutions will bring real value?
2. What is the near-term impact of digital procurement programs?
3. Which digital software vendors will live up to their promises?

We expect procurement to create value from many new applications in the future, considering the function's place at the crossroads of various data flows between the company and its partners. Category managers work with historic and future spending and usage data generated by the company's enterprise resource planning (ERP) and forecasting systems. They receive product specifications provided by their engineering coun-terparts; monitor contract adherence, invoicing behavior, and supplier performance; and generate supplier profiles and scorecards. Procurement also taps into various external data sources, like supply-market-specific time-series data for commodities, currency and inflation rates, tax and tariff data, or supplier solvency data.

But how do companies create real value from this data? In a world of digitalization and with new solutions hitting the market every day, many CPOs are struggling to separate the actual from the fakers.

Procurement is ready for digital transformation. Procurement offices have heavily invested in their technology backbone to improve their transactional capabilities. However, investment into data-driven applica-tions has, so far, been rather small, despite these applications' potential to generate greater returns on investment by improving strategic purchas-ing capabilities. With the pressure to continuously deliver year-over-year savings and diminishing returns from improving transactional capabili-ties, procurement will need to look at improving their digital capabilities to become a full, strategic partner in the organization.

4

SAVING PROCUREMENT FROM ITSELF

Unfortunately, most internal or external customers ask procurement for one thing – to save them money. For old time procurement or purchasing, that was all that mattered. Today, savings goes much deeper. But, there's actually something additional you could save your internal customers that they would value more: time. Why would they value time more than money?

Firstly, the money saved isn't really theirs. It's the organization's money. And while it may be nice for them to be able to accomplish all they need to within a tight budget, saving the organization money won't always make them motivated about how great the procurement department is. They may actually get their budgets reduced if they don't spend it all!

However, saving them time is a more personal benefit. More time breeds less frustration and stress. They'll get to leave work at a decent hour. Their teams will have higher morale. And procurement's customer satisfaction rating will reflect that.

One of the benefits of having higher procurement customer satisfaction is that you will be able to get better cooperation when implementing new procurement initiatives. But, while we have thus far talked about happier internal customers and a more popular procurement department, saving internal customers time has organizational benefits just like lower prices on products and services do.

While saving internal customers time, you can translate those time savings into monetary benefits. For example, if you improve a procurement process where an administrative assistant no longer has to spend five hours a month checking office supply stock and reordering supplies, you can multiply her $15/hour wage by 5 hours by 12 months to get $900 in annual savings. As a result of time savings, paid employee overtime is reduced, open positions are no longer needed to be filled, or headcount is reduced.

There are a number of 'saving procurement' tools one can implement to assist in this project. They are the following and will be discussed in some detail below: procurement savings strategies, procurement savings definitions, procurement savings types, procurement savings reports, procurement savings levers, and procurement savings procurement calculator.

Procurement savings strategies

With the global economy continuing to show positive growth signs, procurement is expanding to keep up with increasing demands worldwide. At the same time, the cut-throat nature of business competition is marking the beginning of a new era of cost cutting, lean management, and operational efficiency. More and more businesses are now geared towards implementing new and improved sourcing practices in order to drive down the bottom line and improve profitability. At the same time, firms are implementing practices that offer the highest return on investment. There is a relatively new trend that procurement managers are following to reassess the sourcing practices. This is known as *spend management* which has five cost savings strategies – creating a road map, using analytics, consolidation and integration, fact-based contract negotiation, and contract compliance tracking.

Creating a detailed roadmap outlines business functions, assigns responsibilities, and coordinates company-wide procurement based on item type or category. Having a clear roadmap is the first step in prioritizing sourcing practices and determining possible points for cost-cutting measure implementation. It also ensures that managers across all departments are aware of the bigger picture and can combine efforts towards achieving their outlined targets.

One way you can channel the power of technology is by analyzing key metrics for all of your product categories and then using this information to make more informed decisions. This includes identifying historical purchasing patterns, demand information, and clear product requirements before negotiating supply.

Supplier consolidation and centralized procurement systems ensure improved integration of your organization in the global supply chain network. You won't wind up with a supply chain disaster on your hands before a big event or major holiday. It also helps in ensuring product availability, customer satisfaction, and most importantly builds brand loyalty and trust

Knowledge of a supplier's pricing policy is also essential. It may be more cost efficient to order a larger volume of a particular product, or place your order sufficiently in advance to get a schedule-based discount. Furthermore, better payment terms based on cash availability can also be negotiated with suppliers.

Even the best organizations fall short when it comes to savings based on contract compliance. Any potential product or service issues that need to be either replaced by the supplier or remedied through further staff training should be identified. Keeping up with these issues and ensuring contract compliance on both ends is one way to avoid costly public battles in the future, and pave the way towards achieving the maximum possible saving potential.

Procurement savings definitions

Please don't be alarmed, I am not going to list definitions. There will be time for that in the glossary. The purpose here is to enlighten procurement to what is at stake in this new age of sourcing.

Want to get a room full of people disagreeing with one another in as little time as possible?

Then ask them all how they define savings in procurement.

The great procurement debate

Procurement is the acquisition of products and/or services from an external source.

But what are procurement savings?

I remember a seminar where various sourcing professionals shared their definitions of what a procurement saving actually was. While there were some common themes, there were still 250+ different definitions of what constituted procurement savings. This is a topic that requires further assessment. An overemphasis on cost savings may lead to purchasing items of reduced quality. While you may have saved on cost, you've also purchased an inferior product. As well as being a questionable definition of a 'saving', this could have many negative ramifications for your organization. These ramifications may even 'wipe out' the value of your savings.

Another problem with an overemphasis on cost savings is that this measure tends to only look at short-term costs, rather than 'life cycle' costs. For example, buying cheaper computer monitors may result in a short-term saving. But if they need to be replaced much earlier than their more expensive counterparts, is this truly a saving in the long term? Procurement cost savings cannot be seen only in the short term, but must also be seen in the bigger picture and/or long term.

Of equal importance is the difference between cost and value. The price of an item should be viewed in terms of both the cost you pay and the outcome you want to achieve.

A perfect example is the procurement of paper. When you need to communicate with others, using paper is one way to achieve this. When you look at procurement from the perspective of the outcome – in this case, allowing communication – you can begin to consider other methods for achieving this. These may cost more in the short term, but less in the long term.

Procurement must balance four factors to achieve the desired outcome of achieving procurement savings. These four factors are: price, quality, quantity, and timelines. A procurement cost saving is only truly a saving when it is achieved by paying a reduced price for a product or service, without reducing or otherwise negatively impacting on the quality, quantity, or timeline.

Procurement savings types

There are two primary methods to achieve procurement savings, and each has a number of types attached to it. One is cost reduction, which includes historical savings, budgetary savings, and technical savings. The other method is cost avoidance, which includes RFP savings, index savings, and ratio savings.

Procurement savings reports

How does a procurement leader know what his or her procurement team is working on? The procurement metrics report should be the answer. That's a simple enough concept. But a common question is: what should be on a procurement report?

I'll share eight items to consider including on your procurement report. That's not to say that these are the only items to include or that each of the items should definitely be included. One should use this as a starting point and edit as one sees fit to suit their procurement department's culture.

Here are the first eight items commonly found on procurement reports:

1. **Cost control performance**. In this section of the report, you should summarize fiscal-year-to-date cost savings, cost savings achieved since the last meeting, cost increases incurred since the last meeting, cost savings opportunities being pursued, and cost increase threats observed.
2. **Sourcing projects**. In this section, you should provide updates on sourcing projects. You may want to consider separating these projects into phases, such as pre-solicitation, awaiting proposals, etc.
3. **Supply risks**. In this section, you should summarize supply risks that you have become aware of. More importantly, you should specify what you are doing to mitigate those risks.
4. **Internal customer collaborations**. Developing relationships with internal customers in the organization is as important a procurement

initiative today as it ever was. In this section, you should share the details of upcoming and recently completed collaborations with internal customers.

5. **Supplier performance reviews**. Every procurement department should be meeting at least annually with its most critical suppliers to review the performance of each. This section of the report should summarize scheduled and completed reviews and share the details on what certain suppliers are doing to improve their performance.

6. **Strategic supplier collaborations**. Beyond just improving their performance on 'the way things are done today', suppliers can provide external ideas for giving your organization a competitive advantage. In this section, you should document these types of ideas that you and your suppliers are implementing and considering for the future.

7. **Process improvements**. Processes don't get better on their own. In fact, if left unmanaged, some processes may tend to get worse or even out of control. In this section, you should share what processes you are evaluating for improvement or actually improving and the gains expected from those improvements.

8. **Value creation efforts**. Today's procurement departments are expected to do more than simply achieve cost savings. They are expected to bring value to the organization in a variety of other ways, such as growing revenue, improving quality, and helping the organization strengthen its brand. A section dedicated to value creation efforts will demonstrate to management that the procurement department is operating in the most modern way.

Procurement savings levers

Levers are basically the drivers that get us to the best procurement value for our products while meeting the growing field of sustainability (more on that subject later).

In this section I will present the four broad procurement value levers. Each of these is based on proven practices by the world's leading organizations. And as we go down the list, each increases in complexity and difficulty in implementation. After briefly introducing each, we'll discuss each one of them, showing their contributions towards procurement goals.

The four areas we explore include:

1. Price-based levers
2. Total cost levers
3. Demand management levers
4. Supply-based levers

Price-based levers are the simplest and most used of the procurement value levers. Focused on getting best pricing for product/service through rigorous competition, this is the easiest to understand and implement. Pricing levers go beyond negotiating the best price and also include increasing spend covered by negotiated contracts. If no one uses a negotiated contract, of course no value is created.

Total cost levers go beyond price and the focus on getting a better 'deal'. Total cost is about looking more broadly at all costs related to procuring and managing a product or service. Ultimately, this is a better measure than best price given most purchases have many other costs beyond price built in. For example, photocopiers have a purchase price as well as a cost associated with maintenance and consumables such as toner and paper over a number of years.

Demand management levers are really just about making sure we don't buy something we don't need. The various approaches include influencing and potentially standardizing specifications, reducing the amount we buy through collaboration with internal stakeholders and suppliers, and driving make-versus-buy decisions.

Supply-based levers provide additional opportunities when applicable. Examples include supplier development, leveraging supplier innovation through collaboration, and restructuring the supply base to better achieve delivered value. All of these levers are predicated on also defining and managing towards socioeconomic goals. Collaboration is important in all four procurement value lever areas.

Procurement savings calculations

Measuring procurement savings, how many hours are spent by organizations every year arguing about what constitutes a saving? Procurement may have one view, finance may have another, the budget holders may hold a different opinion, and the consultants you hired to run a cost reduction program probably have a completely different number.

I'm not going to get into the debate of whether spending less but at a higher price is a saving or spending more but at a lower price is a saving, but here are ten rules of good practice for savings measurement:

1. *Clearly define your savings types and how they are measured.*

   Key factors here are what's permissible as a baseline, especially if there isn't an obvious last price paid, how fluctuating markets are catered for, if at all, how first-time or one-time purchases are measured, and how you handle one-off payments like signing bonuses or volume rebates. There's often no absolute right and wrong, although there is common sense and also good accounting practice.

2. *Be completely aligned with finance.*

   This really goes without saying, but if procurement is to have any credibility in the business when it comes to declaring savings numbers, the CFO needs to at least be in agreement that the savings definitions and measurement methodology are sound.

3. *Reward innovation.*

   It makes me sad when I talk to companies who think measuring purchase price variance is everything there is to measuring savings. Procurement has evolved far beyond simple price reduction and is now much more focused on adding wider value to the business. With this in mind, make sure that the kind of value that can be derived from lateral thinking is measured. What if we don't buy this thing at all because we can do things completely differently, or what if we actually pay more but we get all this great additional service that really helps our efficiency?

4. *Look at the total cost.*

   Following on from rule 3, remember piece price alone is not everything. Make sure delivery, payment terms, supplier management, one-off costs, lifecycle costs, etc. (as far as reasonable), are taken into account when calculating savings.

5. *Understand your cost of capital.*

   $10,000 now is not the same as $10,000 in 12 months' time. Make sure you know the value of a signing bonus compared to a retrospective rebate, and how much lower a price on 15-day-payment terms needs to be to provide better value than a price at 90 days. Knowing the value of your cash will also help of course in negotiations.

6. *Don't stop tracking savings at point of contract. Measure what actually happened.*

   It's a well-documented fact that up to 40% of savings go missing somewhere between the point of contract and the savings actually materializing. Some form of post-contract monitoring and real-time or retrospective adjustment is key to ensuring a decent level of accuracy.

7. *Be accurate, but don't seek perfection.*

   As a balance to rule 6, don't be tempted to take things too far. It can be easy to want to take savings accuracy to the *n*th degree. This might be possible in some instances, depending on technology and particularly on direct materials, but in many cases it's simply not realistic to be 100% accurate across the board. Make a judgment call on effort versus return. With a robust process and the right tools, the high 90%s should be easily achievable.

8. *Don't forget the increases.*

   We all love declaring our cost reductions, but how many of us like to admit our increases? It's a fact of life that these sometimes happen, and we can't completely avoid them no matter how careful we are. If we forget to include these and measure them we only see a distorted picture.

9. *Have a clear governance process.*

   Ensure that savings are approved. The level and type of approval may vary depending on spend, criticality, etc., but it's important that the savings rationale and calculation method are ratified and agreed, to help standardization and provide credibility.

10. *Remember it's a means to an end.*

    The final rule is to keep the big picture in mind. Savings in isolation don't mean a whole lot, in fact they could be bad for the business if reduced spend in certain areas is stifling productivity. It's what those savings bring the business in terms of value that's important, whether it's profit or the ability to spend more to fund growth. It's important to keep this in focus.

5

PROCUREMENT AND SUSTAINABILITY

We have already learned that procurement is the process of finding, acquiring, or buying goods, services, or works from an external source, often via an offer or competitive bids process. The process is used to ensure the buyer receives goods, services, or works at the best possible price, when aspects such as quality, quantity, time, and location are compared. Procurement is considered sustainable when organizations broaden this framework by meeting their needs for goods, services, works, and utilities in a way that achieves value for money and promotes positive outcomes not only for the organization itself but for the economy, environment, and society.

Sustainable procurement is a spending and investment process typically associated with public policy, although it is now applicable in the private sector. Organizations practicing sustainable procurement meet their needs for goods, services, utilities, and works not on a private cost-benefit analysis but with a view to maximizing net benefits for themselves and the wider world. In doing so, they must incorporate extrinsic cost considerations into decisions alongside the conventional procurement criteria of price and quality, although in practice the sustainable impacts of a potential supplier's approach are often assessed as a form of quality consideration. These considerations are typically divided thus: environmental, economic, and social. To procure in a sustainable way involves looking beyond short-term needs and considering the longer-term impacts of each purchase. Sustainable procurement is used to ensure that purchasing reflects broader goals linked to resource efficiency, climate change, and social responsibility.

Sustainable procurement involves a higher degree of collaboration and engagement between all parties in a supply chain. Many businesses have adopted a broad interpretation of sustainable procurement and have developed tools and techniques to support this engagement and collaboration.

The importance of sustainable procurement

Sustainability is an important part of modern society. It's all about making the most of the resources we have, and using those resources in responsible ways. That means procurement has a big role to play.

Sustainable procurement practices vary significantly. Lack of awareness is cited as one of the major challenges, in terms of both processes and outcomes. Yet in a world where organizational reputation is of growing importance, and instant communication means information around such practice is readily available, the increasing need for sustainable practice is clear.

Increasingly, key decisions are being learned by sustainable practice and reputation. Three quarters of consumers rate sustainability as a shopping priority. That means that showing demonstrable sustainability in your business practice and supply chain can have a big impact on your bottom line. That's a huge opportunity for efficient procurement to leverage a significant business advantage.

At the other end of the range sustainable practice is growing in importance in the public sectors. Green government procurement amounted to around $482 million in 2016, showing the increasing focus that the government is placing on sustainable procurement, and the consequent importance of business oversight in tracking and evidencing your own procurement processes.

Like most areas of business, the key to understanding the opportunities that come with sustainability is derived from oversight. That means a transparent system that offers the information you need to understand your own business behavior.

With the ever-increasing growth of e-commerce comes the importance of e-commerce sustainability. Remarkably, e-procurement also provides you the opportunity to demonstrate your sustainable practice. Buyers can create questionnaires for suppliers that help clarify green credentials and sustainable practice, enabling evaluation committees to make informed sustainability decisions. In turn, suppliers are able to easily upload documents such as accreditations or sustainable certificates, demonstrating their own credentials that then feed back into the opportunity for buyers to understand their key suppliers.

Every organization has the opportunity to build a more sustainable business. What e-procurement offers is the ability to understand and evidence those purchasing pathways that empower you to make the right informed decisions, and show that you've done so. When it comes down to the bottom line, better sustainable practice isn't just good for society; it's a clear path towards a more successful business.

To that desired end, of sustainable business practices and environment, companies should be practicing several *principles of sustainable procurement*. The principles are the following:

- **Using procurement to deliver sustainable outcomes** – the procurement document should consider procurement as a strategic process and a way of delivering business objectives through a supply chain. The standard needs to set out how sustainability objectives of an organization are addressed at the early stage of the procurement process through strategic procurement techniques such as market analysis, life cycle assessment, risk management, whole-life costing, product modeling, and social return on investment and more.
- **Sustainable supply not sustainable supplier** – the focus of the standard should be on sustainable supply, not sustainable supplier. This means using procurement techniques to deliver the outcomes required by the buying organization's corporate responsibility objectives.

- **Not one-size-fits-all** – sustainability impacts and risks should be mapped against categories of supply and high priority impacts/categories should be addressed first. This should be done with a wide range of internal stakeholders, also taking into consideration corporate policy and external stakeholder requirements.
- **Manage demand** – the most sustainable way to procure is not to buy at all or to keep demand to a minimum by operating the business more efficiently. There needs to be an organizational link between procurer and user of goods, works, and services.
- **Tier one is not the only one** – must reference management of the overall supply chain where there are often significant risks (such as labor standards) or opportunities (for example, positioning local SMEs in lower tiers of the supply chain).
- **Full and fair opportunity** – local procurement, minority businesses, SMEs, etc., are often significant stakeholder priorities and should be supported through the supply chain where appropriate. However, this needs to be set in the context of full and fair opportunity and not positive discrimination.

Selecting, investigating, and engaging suppliers, contract negotiations, purchase order approvals, etc., procurement processes are often large, unwieldy, and chaotic when many stakeholders are in the mix. Procurement teams are faced with the task of not only managing but also *simplifying* the process in order to reduce expenses and deliver timely results. If your team is struggling under piles of complex manual workflows, procurement management tools could be the automated solution for your procurement ills.

Procurement management tools help those involved in all stages of the procurement process to navigate complex requirements quickly and easily. Instead of tracking swathes of suppliers individually to ensure compliance and performance, procurement management tools enable users to improve internal workflows and tasks.

Ultimately, through automation, procurement management tools streamline purchasing functions for businesses, including:

- Raising and approving purchase orders
- Maintaining inventory

- Supplier onboarding and management
- Receiving and matching invoices and orders

What are the best procurement management tools for your business? The best procurement management tool for your business will depend on the complexity of your firm and the level of functionality you require. Below is a list of five, in no way inclusive, of the possible procurement management tools.

Precoro: a tool which incorporates budget tracking, purchase order approval routing, and supplier onboarding into a feature-rich platform to streamline the procurement lifecycle.

- Users can create customizable reports including spend and analytics, and auto-allocate cost centers, which can be imported into an ERP system.
- Customizable goods and services catalogs and the ability to generate 'free forms' allow users to add granular detail to purchase requests.
- Notifications ensure users are aware of budget overspends.

Coupa: a procurement management tool which manages the whole procurement lifecycle, including approval workflows, inventory management, and budget management.

- Users are able to manage approvals from email and the mobile app.
- Coupa integrates with ERP systems such as NetSuite and SAP Business One.
- It allows visibility of invoices within the approval and payment process.

Promena e-Sourcing: a sourcing and procurement platform that aims to make the purchasing process simpler. Requests for information (RFIs), requests for proposal (RFPs), and requests for quotation (RFQs) can be handled with Promena e-Sourcing, along with an e-procurement module.

- A main dashboard enables users to manage procurement, sourcing, and transactional activity.
- The Promena Supplier Relationship Management (SRM) tool allows users to collate supplier information, assist with risk management, and create online reverse and forward auctions.

eBuyerAssist Procurement: it is a modular procurement solution, covering RFQs, RFIs, invoice matching, inventory control, and much more. Users can also manage warehouses, contracts, and strategic sourcing with eBuyerAssist Procurement.

- Users are able to choose and pay for only the modules they need, e.g. requisitioning or vendor portals.
- eBuyerAssist Procurement integrates with accounting solution QuickBooks and ERP solution Microsoft Dynamics AX.
- Users can assess vendor risk management through auditing their suppliers.

Workplace requisition and procurement: a procurement solution suitable for organizations from 5 users to 4,000 users. Job costing, budgeting, and reporting are all included in the platform, as well as a self-service portal for vendors.

- Users have access to a project approval engine and an advanced budgeting engine for real-time general ledger budget validation.
- The software integrates with ERP systems Intacct and Microsoft Dynamics GP.

Procurement is indisputably at a crossroads. It is increasingly under pressure to move beyond its traditional role and become a strategic contributor to business outcomes. A definite vision of the 'procurement of tomorrow' is emerging, and it looks a lot different from the procurement of today. How do we get from where we are today to what will be required tomorrow? In other words, how are we to realize the procurement of the future?

6

PROCUREMENT SOLUTIONS IN
THE DIGITAL AGE

Emerging digital and advanced analytics tools promise new levels of procurement performance. To deliver that promise, chief procurement officers (CPOs) must discover which of them are best suited to the needs of their companies.

Big data and advanced analytics will have profound implications in raising data-driven decision making to a new level, helping companies to generate new insights, and enabling them to collaborate at appropriate levels. Imagine a procurement team so deeply connected to every tier of its supply base that it has access to all relevant data on cost structures, supply availability, lead times, financial and operational risks, and service and quality metrics. This procurement team would be well-positioned to negotiate the 'right' prices, instantaneously adapt its own planning, or switch to alternative suppliers in the event of supply shortages. It could even proactively help suppliers improve deteriorating quality levels by spotting problems earlier and identifying their root causes more accurately.

CPOs are also asking *which* of the new digital solutions will bring real value to their companies today. Which of the many 'digital procurement' software vendors will live up to their promises? What should their company's roadmap for digital procurement look like?

We expect procurement to create value from many new applications in the future, considering the function's place at the crossroads of various data flows between the company and its partners. Category managers work with historic and future spending and usage data generated by the company's enterprise resource planning (ERP) and forecasting systems. They receive product specifications provided by their engineering counterparts; monitor contract adherence, invoicing behavior, and supplier performance; and generate supplier profiles and scorecards. Procurement also taps into various external data sources, like supply-market-specific time-series data for commodities, currency and inflation rates, tax and tariff data, or supplier solvency data.

But how do companies create real value from this data? In a world of digital hype and with new solutions hitting the market every day, many CPOs are struggling to separate the hard core facts from the tease. The digital applications that will make a real difference to a company's procurement performance fall into two broad sections: tools that *identify and create value* and tools that *prevent value loss*.

Advanced spend intelligence and automated sourcing insights are examples of the first type of tool. Spend visibility tools begin with solutions that pull historic purchase order and invoice data, and create a spend budget. The prevalence of fragmented ERP systems means many multinational and multi-business companies still find it difficult to build even simple spend budgets. Some companies, however, are already automating data cleanup and classification with algorithms that make use of artificial intelligence and self-learning methods.

We expect that the solutions currently available in the market will be further enriched with additional data sources and the inclusion of basic, category-level key performance indicators (KPIs). For example, they will be able to generate automated price and specification benchmarks across entities, or facility management costs per square foot. Category managers will have automatically generated dashboards and heat maps at their fingertips, helping them identify and capture sourcing opportunities. Finally, by linking the spend-category-level solution to company budgets and profit and loss planning data in real-time, next-generation systems will help reach procurement of the future.

Collaborative and advanced sourcing are examples of the second type of tool. While many systems support transactional procurement processes, very few work-flow solutions currently support the generation of comprehensive category strategies and the systematic identification of savings drivers. There are emerging solutions that are able to guide category managers through a configurable an early stage process that includes every step in the creation of a category strategy: understanding demand, analyzing the market, generating savings, and measuring the effectiveness of implementation. Relevant target meetings with cross-functional partners will be triggered automatically, and all ideas will be stored and tracked up to the final implementation steps.

These work-flow solutions will allow teams to collaborate via shared file spaces, chats and video calls, and superiors will be able to track category manager activities and their impact in real time. As they serve as structured storehouses for all the analyses conducted and insights generated during the strategy development process, these work-flow systems also will make the assembly of category strategy documents and negotiation preparation packs almost automatic.

Many of today's more advanced category analytics are already very well standardized: for example, total cost of ownership calculations for high volumes of similar parts, like fasteners or motors. These analyses will increasingly be coded into standard applications. Once defined, these category solutions will routinely create the defined analyses, and automatically flag potential improvements and specific levers needed to capture them.

Knowing what a part or service *should cost* when produced at maximum efficiency and effectiveness is a key weapon for every buyer when negotiating with vendors. The cleansheet approach used to calculate such costs can also help to identify opportunities for savings from changes to a product's design or its value chain. Cleansheet tools comprise a work-flow application to build calculation sheets, several expert tools to estimate different cost areas like machining, logistics, or overhead cost, and a set of databases containing template libraries and factor costs (e.g. labor rates, raw material index prices, and currencies).

Early involvement with internal customers and cross-functional cooperation to jointly challenge demand, specifications, and processes is critical for good sourcing. Digital platforms that foster exchange, transparency, and interaction can facilitate that collaboration. A number of large software vendors already provide generic collaborative spaces, including file repositories, collaborative workspaces, audio- and video-conferences, and calendaring. We expect to see the emergence of solutions that are specifically geared toward the requirements of strategic sourcing, allowing for timely and effective interactions to challenge what, where, and how to source.

Procure-to-pay solutions were among the first digital tools available to support operational and tactical procurement activities. Since their introduction in the early 2000s, they have evolved significantly in functionality, covering an increasing scope of the end-to-end process, from sourcing to payment of the suppliers, and extending from requisition management to adjacent areas like expense management.

The procure-to-pay tools of the future will use the vast amount of order and invoice transaction data available to enable value generation in core operational activities. They will create prophetic order configurations for repeat buyers, reducing processing time and encouraging the use of standard order templates. They will also automatically identify potential suppliers for categories not covered by contracts or catalogues, supporting operational buyers by creating more competition.

For many companies, especially those with global manufacturing and service footprints, value loss is still one of the main untapped sources of procurement shock. Advanced compliance management tools will act as a vigilant watchdog, scanning every procurement transaction, both from structured ERP systems and unstructured sources like invoices or expenses, to identify and quantify the losses, and actively drive their resolution.

Advanced compliance management will be especially useful in the case of large, high-value outsourcing contracts, which are often governed by complex legal frameworks and dozens of individual service line agreements and KPIs. Future systems will automatically extract all these conditions from contracts through machine reading and match them against continuous streams of invoices, supplier activity, and performance data. Category managers, buyers, and business owners will then be alerted about compliance breaches and their business impact. The value at stake here is huge, considering the level of leakage of the life of a typical contract, and the high level of manual effort currently applied to contract governance.

Supplier performance management systems will deliver real-time insights on supplier performance, gaps, along with anticipated cost, quality, or delivery-time issues. Similarly, they will also link to automated scope and service-level monitoring systems and offer integrated claims management functionality. The availability of this information will allow category managers to act more quickly and decisively when problems occur, and will give them the tools they need to encourage suppliers to improve.

Measuring the performance of the procurement organization as a whole and on an individual category level is the last application where we see significant room for improvement using digital tools. Systems like the category strategy work-flow portal described above will log all the activities of the strategic sourcing team, and savings ideas will be tracked in parallel. This information will allow the CPO to oversee and manage progress and results, even down to a category manager's task level if required. Future work-flow solutions will embed these performance management features to manage group, category, and individual performance on a real-time basis.

To decide which of these solutions are right for them, companies need to understand the specific value drivers offered by each, and assess their potential impact on their own processes and teams. Those value drivers include higher efficiency per transaction, superior insights leading to better negotiation results, or lower risks through improved foresight. Many applications address several value drivers at the same time, although to a different extent. The ultimate impact of each driver will also be company-specific, depending, for example, on transaction volumes, the categories sourced, and the sophistication of the company's people and other current processes.

A natural place to start the journey toward reaping the benefits of end-to-end digitization, advanced analytics, and automation are the following three areas. First, companies should conduct a thorough diagnostic of the current tool landscape for the sourcing company. Second, they should establish the need for action based on a clear set of KPIs. Finally, they must have a clear understanding of the opportunities at stake both from existing tools and from solutions yet to be developed.

Will these new tools automate the category manager's or procurer's job in the future? I believe just the opposite will occur. Many of the tools described above allow much more thorough analysis and deep investigation to create more impact. Such tools will only deliver their true value in the hands of capable talent. Companies should start building the required talent and exploring the promises of digital procurement solutions today. Many tools are still in their infancy. Ultimately, only by experimenting and building on their initial successes can CPOs determine which digital procurement solutions will help them create the next level of value for their companies.

Part 3

SUPPLY CHAIN LOGISTICS

One of the often missing links, however, in supply chain visibility is transportation management. Basically it means the act of getting the needed finished goods from start location to destination. We call this the transportation supply chain.

Logistics refers to the movement of product from one location to another as it makes its way from the beginning of a supply chain to the customer's handle. This requires a new broad look at the business of transportation supply chain, including supply chain management, logistics, and procurement. A large portion of a company's supply chain costs come from transportation/logistics. Thus, it is imperative to understand how logistics costs fit into the firm's business plan. As the logistics manager thinks more about the role of transportation in the overall supply chain and business, and less about the tactics of transportation, one can strategically work with other players in the supply chain in order to more effectively reach the corporate and business vision their organization has set out to reach.

Many manufacturers and retailers have found that they can use state-of-the-art supply chain management to reduce inventory and warehousing costs while speeding up delivery to the end customer.

Any supply chain's success is closely linked to the appropriate use of transportation. Walmart has effectively used a quick-to-respond logistical system to lower its overall costs. At distribution centers, Walmart uses cross-docking, a process in which products are exchanged between trucks so that each truck going to a retail store has products from different suppliers.

Managers should ensure that a firm's logistics/transportation strategy supports its competitive strategy. Firms should evaluate the transportation function based on a combination of transportation costs, other costs such as inventory affected by transportation decisions, and the level of responsiveness achieved with customers.

1

WHAT IS LOGISTICS?

There is confusion and mishandling of the terms 'logistics' and 'supply chain' in many areas. Logistics is *not* the same as supply chain. Logistics is the management of the movement of goods, whereas supply chain management covers the many other areas we're discussing here.

But logistics is a part of supply chain and that means whoever manages your supply chain will be responsible for managing freight forwarders, shipping companies, parcel delivery companies (like FedEx and UPS), customs brokers, and third-party logistics providers (3PL).

Logistics providers should be managed in the same way that you would manage your suppliers. Costs and contracts can be negotiated. You can source suppliers of the products you need. Shipping and warehousing costs can be one of the largest expenses in your supply chain, and it's critical that your logistics providers are measured and managed to control those costs.

When a company creates a logistics strategy, it is defining the service levels at which its organization is at its most cost-effective. Because supply chains are constantly changing and evolving, a company may develop a number of logistics strategies for specific product lines, specific countries, or specific customers.

Remember, the ultimate goal of any logistics strategy is to deliver what your customers want and when they want it – and getting that done by spending as little money as possible. That means working with your logistics partners throughout your supply chain.

The supply chain constantly changes and that will affect any logistics organization. To adapt to the flexibility of the supply chain, companies should develop and implement a formal logistics strategy. This will allow a company to identify the impact of imminent changes and make organizational or functional changes to ensure service levels are not reduced. An organization can start to develop a logistics strategy by researching four distinct levels of their logistics organization.

- **Strategic**: by examining the company's objectives and strategic supply chain decisions, the logistics strategy should review how the logistics organization contributes to those high-level objectives.
- **Structural**: the logistics strategy should examine the structural issues of the logistics organization, such as the optimum number of warehouses and distribution centers, or what products should be produced at a specific manufacturing plant.
- **Functional**: any strategy should review how each separate function in the logistics organization is to achieve functional excellence.
- **Implementation**: the key to developing a successful logistics strategy is how it is to be implemented across the organization. The plan for implementation will include development or configuration of an information system, introduction of new policies and procedures, and the development of a change management plan.

Along with the above four levels of strategy come a number of components of that operation that need to be examined in the context of the strategy to ascertain whether any potential cost benefits can be achieved. There are different component areas for each company, but the list should at least include the following:

- **Transportation**: does the current transportation strategies help service levels?

- **Outsourcing**: what outsourcing is used in the logistics function? Would a partnership with a third-party logistics company improve service levels?
- **Logistics systems**: do the current logistics systems provide the level of data that is required to successfully implement a logistics strategy, or are new systems required?
- **Competitors**: review what the competitors offer. Can changes to the company's customer service improve service levels?
- **Information**: is the information that drives the logistics organization real-time and accurate? If the data is inaccurate then the decisions that are made will be in error.
- **Strategy review**: are the objectives of the logistics organization in line with company objectives and strategies?

A successfully implemented logistics strategy is important for companies that are dedicated to keeping service levels at the highest levels possible despite changes that occur in the supply chain. The goal of any logistics strategy is to make sure you and your company are delivering to your customers what they want and when they want it. By following these guidelines, you can ensure that your logistics are aligned with your customers' needs, your inventory targets, and your company's cost-reduction goals.

Your company may need to review its logistics strategy from time to time, as supply chains and supply chain priorities change. If your supplier base had been primarily located in the United States and Mexico, and now, because of a change in your supply chain, your suppliers are now primarily located in Asia, you'll need to review your existing logistics strategy.

The same transportation and freight forwarding providers you were using may not be the right strategic partners for that kind of supply chain realignment. Define your service-level goals and value stream map your current logistics landscape in order to determine what needs to be changed.

2

LOGISTICS IN THE 21ST CENTURY

Though we have just begun the new millennium, the significant pull of globalization – new trading partners, cheaper supply sources, and emerging markets – is compelling enterprises of all sizes to build alliances and online commerce systems that efficiently deliver products to customers while providing a worldwide view of operations. Virtual along with leading-edge and traditional organizations are developing new strategies to track orders and react to changes in real time and transportation of materials as they move across the supply chain from supplier to customer.

The goal is to electronically link the entire sales, production, and delivery process into one seamless flow of information across international borders and time zones. Having a global view of logistic movements enables better decision making and reduces costs, while providing a means for sharing information among trading partners. This type of visibility and collaboration provides bottom-line benefits along with an improved ability to react to customer requirements.

The global nature of the Internet is showing how orders will be fulfilled in the next century. The Internet is also making it easier to find and do business with small and midsize suppliers, particularly in remote areas of the world. Because this technology is open to all, the advantage large, multi-national enterprises have traditionally held regarding the movement of goods is being challenged.

There's a growing recognition that an improved flow of information and the ability to react, in real time, to a changing demand-and-supply situation is necessary to be a leading supplier or retailer. This naturally entails close coordination with transportation and other partners in the fulfillment of orders.

Companies have traditionally monitored major trading lanes across the country or around the world, but this is no longer enough to insure a high level of customer service. To keep up, logistic systems must encompass a solution that automates the process of dealing with customers, such as order revisions and document management. In addition, tracking shipments, handling payments, and monitoring inventory positions (by item and location) across the supply chain is necessary.

Transportation and fulfillment providers, including FedEx Express, UPS, SeaLand, and DHL, are opening up their systems, allowing e-commerce vendors to access, track, and communicate logistics information in a variety of innovative ways. Webcasting and publish/subscribe techniques allow all interested parties to be alerted to situations requiring attention. This includes changes in customer demand, order revisions/cancellations, and, often most difficult to resolve, adjustments in quantity and/or location for deliveries in progress.

Transportation networks and the software used to track shipments must minimize the movement of goods via Internet-based collaborative relationships. Improving visibility into individual logistic events reduces delivery time while lowering transportation costs. The ability to alter the movement of goods, in real time, is a significant customer service advantage. Inbound and or outbound freight planning must be coordinated with the order management processes. Close operational collaboration with customers and suppliers provides for dynamic decision opportunities.

Dynamic decision opportunities are the logistics holy grail. Order fulfillment via the transfer of freight across the supply chain involves thousands of joint and individual inventory movements. A percentage of these movements are unnecessary and potentially counter-productive as they don't take into account the latest logistics picture. A collaborative e-commerce system with visibility into the supply chain can recommend revised inventory movements along with associated operational changes. This includes notifications to affected suppliers, transportation partners and, of course, customers.

Most businesses focus on the supply side of the logistics equation because that's where they can exert more influence. It's easier to control the purchasing of supplies than to evaluate and react to the customer side of the value chain. However, forward-looking companies recognize the advantages of improving the demand side of the equation. Internet-based e-commerce solutions are adept at addressing these issues as they tend to be customer-focused and order management-oriented.

Integrating incoming supplies from vendors with outgoing shipments to customers requires globally accessible applications that coordinate both front-office and back-office activities, including information from transportation and fulfillment partners. Whether there is a central data storehouse or data is distributed across the Internet is a question of structural design and collaborative trading relationships.

Strategic decisions of the future will be based on up-to-date, real-time logistic events that are shared across the value chain and accessed via the Web. As more industries become commoditized, commercial success becomes a matter of branding and efficient, economical response to a customer's changing requirements.

As customers have increased the demands placed on suppliers, the onus falls on suppliers to provide more sophisticated solutions within the same cost constraints. When order volumes increase, suppliers must work faster and more efficiently. When customers ask for special labels, bar codes, packaging, and other value-added services, as well as complex distribution and logistics conditions, manufacturers must pay extra attention to detail to maintain accuracy and streamline the entire order cycle. Achieving these customer-focused objectives requires the integration of operational, tactical, and strategic functions across the trading horizon.

An integrated logistics solution can tell when the warehouse is short of product and also locate the source of a problem, whether it's due to an en-route delivery, warehouse situation, or change to the scope of an order. As the movement towards pull-driven manufacturing, make-to-order, and mass customization increases, suppliers must focus on improving customer service through better execution, not simply through improved planning.

Companies strive to increase responsiveness to customer's needs by meeting their requirements for getting the right product to the right place at the right time. A manufacturer, retailer or distributor must react quickly to problems, remain flexible, and provide value-added services in order to maintain and increase its customer base.

Fully integrated logistics system also considers order consolidation, traffic patterns, and routes, but has visibility across multiple sites. The system looks at actual inventory in real time at distribution sites, warehouses, and in transit across a supply chain to better meet demands placed on each facility. It also allows users to reroute and replan based on a trading partner's ability to deliver on time. When a problem arises alternative suppliers or transportation options must be determined even if that means splitting an order.

Making appropriate deployment decisions without knowing order levels and inventory numbers is difficult and unlikely to provide an optimal solution. Order management is not enough if it is not integrated into the delivery and transportation backbone. The grand vision of almost every organization that initiates an Internet-based, collaborative e-commerce solution is to be constantly in line with their logistics environment in order to satisfy customer demand without wasting precious resources such as time, labor, dollars, or material. Such operational efficiency leads to consistent delivery of high-quality, low-cost goods backed by superior customer service, all of which give a company a competitive edge within its marketplace while enhancing its brand with trading partners

Orders are being fulfilled every minute of every day. Having the visibility of transportation moves and being able to react to changes is key to meeting tight customer delivery windows. As global competition intensifies, especially from virtual organizations, enterprises must avoid increased order cycle time and cost, as well as heightened sensitivity to customer service levels and in-transit visibility. Because customer service requirements drive every decision, customer satisfaction can be increased through on-time deliveries of the right products to the right locations. The intelligent use of 24/7-available, e-commerce systems allows an enterprise to proactively respond to exceptions. Costs are minimized and customer responsiveness increases in proportion to resolving the exception as close to its real-time occurrence as possible. This is not a trivial issue and one that will require investment and coordination if true benefits are to be achieved.

Companies must learn to trust their business partners. There is a very real — and sometimes justified — fear that information sharing can turn into a competitive disadvantage. But trading partners that exchange information on a regular basis are better able to work as a single entity. Together, they have a greater understanding of the end customer and are, therefore, better able to respond to changes in the marketplace. These companies also realize they must harness the power of technology to collaborate with their business partners as never before. Using a new breed of logistics awareness, e-commerce applications provide the most intuitive, open, and cost-effective methods for communicating information among organizations involved in a trade.

In addition to order and fulfillment information defect rates, engineering changes, and product enhancements can also be shared. Buyers, suppliers, and transportation partners that remain in constant communication reduce their margin for error and best manage expectations. Partners can also collaborate, in real time, on product designs and enhancements. Trust increases because all trading partners reap the benefits of faster cycle times, reduced inventory, and the improved movement of goods. Ultimately, the customer gets a higher-quality product at a lower price. E-commerce websites can also create a trading community where partners from around the world can exchange information to further optimize this virtual value chain. The Internet is the core to all of this as it provides the capacity to improve the flow of information, eliminate paper-based functions, and link organizations, locally or globally.

Logistics functionality and the integration with logistics partners must be done in phases. Initially, customers must be provided with real-time, seamless integration to shipping/tracking systems, and shippers must be provided with notification at the time the order is approved.

This functionality includes ship rate, track number, order status, and track line item. As the trading relationship grows, shipment estimation, shipping method selection, advanced shipping notice (ASN), and cancel shipment functionality is added. Online dispatch requests to ship product from supplier to customer or in reverse must also be implemented in a cost-effective manner.

Traditional return processes are inefficient, costly to maintain, involve long cycle times, and are difficult to track. The integration of e-commerce systems with shipment vendors give businesses better control over the return of merchandise, while increasing service levels to customers. This includes complex tasks like recalls, upgrades or repairs, trade-ins, and refunds. Eventually, all logistics and service-related functions will be provided online and coordinated throughout the trading community.

As we head deeper into the 21st century, business as usual is anything but that, as businesses move to capture the competitive advantages offered by the Internet and the collaborative communication amongst trading partners. One of the keys to success is an efficient and flexible logistics model that ties buyers to sellers throughout the order process and fulfillment cycles. This means coordinating information from acquisition of raw materials to after-sales service.

3

PHYSICAL AND DIGITAL SUPPLY CHAINS ARE MERGING

Before we approach the actual merging of these 'two' supply chains, we should define what is meant by a digital supply chain. You may have heard the term 'digital supply chain management' being used to describe an emerging business function. But what exactly is a digital supply chain, and how is one supposed to manage it?

Depending on the context in which it's used, the term 'digital supply chain' could have one of two different meanings:

1. The digital aspects of a physical supply chain
2. The chain of technology companies involved in the delivery of digital products

In the first definition, 'digital supply chain' is typically used when discussing how the development and implementation of advanced digital technologies (IoT, blockchain, machine learning, artificial intelligence, predictive analytics, etc.) can drive improvements to traditional supply chains.

Who's responsible for managing the digital supply chain? It is the same team responsible for any supply chain functions (which could be sales, manufacturing, logistics, etc.).

These teams are tasked with finding new ways to accomplish the same goals they've always had: improving efficiency and increasing margins. In other words, 'digital supply chain management' is really just supply chain management with the added layer of technologies. These technologies include, but are not limited to,

- Predictive analytics to optimize inventory allocation and forecast demand
- Automated replenishment solutions
- Robotics to speed up assembly or picking
- IoT sensors to gather real-time feedback from manufacturing equipment and vehicle

Digital technology is disrupting traditional operations and now every business is a digital business. The impact on supply chain management is particularly great. Businesses cannot unlock the full potential of digital without re-inventing their supply chains.

Stronger links between goods in the supply chain and the data that surrounds them are opening up exciting opportunities for supply chain logistics. Some 94% of supply chain executives expect to receive more real-time data from their distribution networks in the next five years. This expected jump in viable information is due to a published report from the International Chamber of Commerce – 'Rethinking Trade and Finance' – which states that the physical and digital supply chains are rapidly merging.

Corporations such as Caterpillar and Levi Strauss & Co are tying together advanced technology to better understand their global supply networks and respond to changes in demand or disruptions in the supply chain in real time, by connecting the physical supply chain to the data supply chain.

Meanwhile, Levi Strauss & Co uses a cloud platform to create a sharper picture of its suppliers, enabling it to identify its most ethical partners. Acting on that data, it began to provide lower-cost working capital to suppliers with the highest labor, safety, and environmental standards.

The better companies get at understanding the data throughout their supply network and acting upon it, the more agile and responsive they will become – ultimately helping to keep up with some of the unpredictability and consistent change that comes with global business right now.

Strategically, the alignment between expectations emerging in the market, the ocean of data that will enable rich analysis, and the technological capabilities to undertake analysis, as well as design and deploy solutions, is converging in a transformational way.

The linkages between supply chain visibility, traceability, and the growing desire to conduct business on a sustainable basis are clear and growing, with implications yet to be fully appreciated, but it is clear that finance – specifically trade-related financing – can be an important enabler of these developments.

The major thrust of this merger is what, in the industry, is called the 'fourth industrial revolution'. The first industrial revolution began in the 1780s with the introduction of water and steam-powered mechanical production facilities. Approximately 30 years later, the first electricity-powered assembly line was constructed in 1870, heralding the second industrial revolution. This facilitated the development of mass production, a revolution responsible for bringing development of the many products on which we rely on in our daily lives.

In the late 1960s, the first programmable logistics controller (PLC) Modicon 084 was developed. This device enabled production automation through the use of electronic and information systems and initiated the third industrial revolution.

Today we are witnessing the birth of the fourth industrial revolution, commonly referred to as Industry 4.0 in our time, or the advent of digital transformation. Today's technology innovation impact is pervasive and creating massive change. Today, physical systems such as robotics and machines are able to be controlled by automation systems that utilize machine learning algorithms, requiring only minimal input from human operators.

Industry 4.0 is an ongoing evolution in the revolutionary processes that have changed and shaped the world, enabling greater sharing of information in real time and collaboration. The concept of Industry 4.0 brings together the digital and physical worlds. Using information technology and operations technology, the supply chain can be transformed from a sequential system to an open, interconnected system (a digital supply chain).

Information technology, data analytics, and business intelligence are transforming the business landscape and changing the way we live, make decisions, and interact with the world. From smart watches and other IoT devices to 3-D printers, autonomous vehicles, and intelligent robots that wash our floors and produce our goods to drones, technology is everywhere. We are interfacing with our world via sensors that are continually collecting data that is then analyzed and used for a wide variety of purposes. Look out for the end of traditional business models.

Is the digital supply chain transformation the new reality? If it is two questions should be asked.

1. How imminent is the evolution of the digital supply chain?
2. Are supply chains actually planning for this?

Perhaps the answer lies within the next few sections.

The more that these technologies are used in concert, the stronger, more resilient and responsive the digital supply chain network will be. The digital supply chain will enable companies to compete more effectively and will provide advantages including efficiency gains, decreased time and labor costs, and much more.

As the supply chain becomes increasingly digital, the 'rough edges' will wear off. Increased visibility will provide transparency into the needs and challenges of supply chain network partners. Because the entire supply chain environment will be fully integrated and digital data will flow seamlessly, supply and demand signals will initiate at any point in the network and be able to travel in real time throughout the environment. *This will change supply chain logistics networks*! If there is a shortage of a raw material, sudden influx of consumer demand due to a 'hot' new trendy product or supply chain disruption due to a natural phenomenon, the entire network will know about it in real time and be able to react accordingly.

Companies will need to invest in a range of digital technologies including the cloud, big data, IoT, virtual reality, and more to enable new business models and facilitate the transformation to real-time, shared data. Through digital transformation and integration of every link across supply chains, enterprises will find new ways to operate, inter-relate, and do business. A complete, holistic view of the supply chain will be enabled, facilitating more natural collaboration and responsiveness from business to business and business to consumer. As new technologies such as big data analytics, the cloud, and IoT are increasingly adopted, consumers, employees, and businesses are increasingly forcing companies to develop more responsive and reliable supply chains. With these technologies will come a new generation of supply chain professionals – ones that are completely knowledgeable in how to integrate, maintain, and upgrade these technologies into a smooth running 'machine'. A completely different process of recruitment of supply chain professionals will be necessary.

Digital supply chain management will be an everyday reality and traditional business models will become outdated. Making the digital supply chain work will necessitate a shift in the culture of organizations. Get ready for transformation! By harnessing the power of the digital supply chain and its elements, companies will be able to benefit from tremendous advantages in flexibility, efficiency, cost reduction, and customer service. Using digital technologies, business models will be altered, processes will be altered, and new opportunities and means of producing revenue will be uncovered and developed.

Although digitalization involves greater investment of time, labor, and resources, the rewards are higher. Digitalization forces companies to go back to basics, to review the value proposition, not simply operational processes. The point of digitalization is to deliver better products, services, and an enhanced customer experience.

Whether your business operates narrowly in North America or across the globe, the digital supply chain will undoubtedly have an impact on your company. The world is undergoing another massive transformation, to the fourth industrial revolution so you better get ready. The new prototype unites the digital world with that of the physical world. Using new information technology devices, IoT, IoS, augmented reality, 3-D printing, cloud computing, and other innovations, the industrial world is being transformed so that data can be shared, visualized, and made transparent in real time.

Using digitization in combination with a wide array of new information systems and resources enables companies to collaborate, become proactive, and interact internally and with other organizations to become more efficient and produces tremendous cost-, time-, and labor-saving benefits. All of this leads to a desirous effect: the ability for companies to compete on the global stage.

According to industry experts, the digital supply chain has been forming for years. As 3PLs, warehouse operators, and distribution centers utilize radio frequency barcode scanners, mobile computers, and warehouse management systems to process goods and streamline inventory management operations, they are operating in the digital world. The same is true for warehouses and third-party logistics providers that use RFID, EDI, and WMS. The difference is the new bond between partners across the supply chain network using cloud computing solutions to transmit data comprehensively and in real time throughout the digital supply chain ecosystem.

The digitization of supply chain management networks continues to increase. More companies are investing in new information technology tools, resources, and skilled workers to implement the vision of a connected world. It may seem intimidating, but the digital transformation will help businesses to be more agile, respond more quickly, and operate more efficiently.

4

21ST-CENTURY DIGITAL LOGISTICAL SOLUTIONS

The garage startup has become as much of an American legend in the 21st century as the automobile and the drive-in were to earlier generations. The idea that anyone with an idea can change the world is as romantic as democracy itself, but it's not altogether true. A garage startup only works if there is existing technology to build on top of.

The problem is that every technology eventually runs out of steam. When that happens, progress will grind to a halt without a significant breakthrough. As technology becomes more complex, that type of advancement becomes so hard to achieve that it becomes out of reach for any single organization, much less a few guys in a garage.

The 21st century can also be considered a new era of innovation, which will create insightful new technologies, classes of data, and business models. It is likely to be the most important change we have seen in the last half a century.

To understand the size of the shift, imagine yourself as the CEO of a Dow component company, circa 1918. The impacts of the major technological forces that will shape the 20th century are not yet clear, but their capacity for disruption will be so great that your company has only roughly 50% chance of surviving the next decade.

The burgeoning forces at work today may be just as profound, and it's critically important to begin to explore and understand them because they will shape business models for decades to come. Much like a century ago, it will not be enough to simply wait to see their impact and adapt. If you want to win the future, it will require shaping it now.

The past few decades have been dominated by the digital revolution, and it seems like things have been moving very fast. If you walked into an average 1950s-era household, you would see much that you would recognize, including home appliances, a TV, and an automobile. On the other hand, if you had to live in a 1900s-era home, with no running water or electricity, you would struggle to survive.

Now we're entering a new era of innovation that is likely to be far more impactful. Much like the computer revolution was built on top of electricity, the new era will use computing to drive advancement in other fields, such as genomics, nanotechnology, and robotics, to spur innovation in industries like energy, manufacturing, and medicine.

This new era has already begun. We are learning to manipulate individual atoms and molecules as well as to work with massive amounts of data and create machines that can do jobs previously thought to be uniquely human. Still, much like our predecessors in 1918, we are unable to fully grasp what the impact will be.

Data used to be backward looking. We would input critical information in a ledger or file, store it in a shelf or a cabinet and take it out when the need arose. Computers allowed us to move data into virtual folders, which helped us clean up our desks considerably, but for the most part, we used information in the same way.

Today's technologies allow us to collect data in real time and apply it to the real world through the use of advanced analytics and predictive modeling. Open data for science is beginning to transform how new discoveries are made, altering accepted wisdom of scientific method. These are important developments in and of themselves, but what's really exciting is the potential to apply new technologies and new data to the creation of completely new business models.

Let's return to 1918 and think about what the world looked like then. Electricity and the automobile were gaining ground, but the first major impacts wouldn't arrive till the next decade. Secondary technologies, like household appliances, radio communications, highways, and shopping malls, created further revolutions. Quantum theory was still a decade away.

To the typical executive in 1918, none of this would have made any sense, but these technologies would let loose a completely different business environment that most firms were ill-equipped to handle. The only Dow components that survive today in any recognizable form are AT&T, B.F. Goodrich, Western Union, and Westinghouse – all firms that benefited from the new technology.

Today we can only see a small slice of what the future holds for us. We know that computer architecture, energy sources, and manufacturing practices will change dramatically and we can see rough outlines of the shift already. What we can't see is the secondary effects – the technologies and business models that will be built on top of base technologies – that will impact today's industries.

No newspaperman looked at a mainframe computer and saw social media or a website, just like no shop owner looked at a 'horseless carriage' and saw a supermarket. They were too busy trying to serve their customers and beat their competitors, so missed the growing threat that would disrupt their businesses.

That's why today it is crucially important to set aside resources to explore, experiment, and seize challenges so that we can begin to understand and eventually channel the forces that will shape any industry. It's better to prepare than to adapt because by the time you see the need to adapt, it may already be too late.

Part 4

INVENTORY MANAGEMENT IN THE AGE OF DIGITAL AUTOMATION

A prominent inventory is considered a core component of the supply chain and is where all areas of the supply chain come together in tandem. In this section we will explore why inventory management in supply chain is the key to sustained success.

Inventory can be a company's most important asset. Every company, regardless of the type of inventory, needs to establish these five steps to begin a journey of inventory visibility.

1. Determine where the inventory exists across your network and systems that are tracking that inventory.
2. Decide whether you are going to build or buy.
3. Decide if you are going to update your entire order management system or start with getting an accurate real-time view of your inventory.
4. Build a business case to justify the investment.
5. Start assessing different vendors to observe which is the best fit for your needs.

Inventory fulfillment is at the heart of the customer experience and gets to what really matters. It drives loyalty and ensures customers return to your business. In order to grow, it's important to keep the promises you make and deliver orders efficiently. It's vital that companies with complex supply chains and manufacturing processes strike the right balance of inventory size.

1

HOW AI SOLVES THE RIDDLE OF INVENTORY MANAGEMENT

The problems that perplex inventory management are well known: excess inventory languishing in warehouses, millions of dollars tied up in working capital, and stock shortages that erode margins and hurt brand image. Companies face hefty penalties from buyers if they can't meet thresholds in service-level contracts on time and in full.

The solution, however, has remained elusive – and not for lack of effort or investment. World wide, corporations employ thousands of planners and spend millions of dollars on alphabet soup of software to manage inventory and other links in the supply chain, from ERP, MES, MRP, CRM, and WMS to planning and logistics tools.

Organizations are confronted by massive quantities of data that multiply by the minute, across every function that affects inventory management – planning, procurement, production, distribution, and fulfillment. Contracting with channel partners for some of those processes complicates the challenge.

Those siloed functions make holistic visibility nearly impossible to achieve with standard applications and Excel spreadsheets. When the problem arises, it could take days or weeks to pinpoint the root cause – that one weak link that disrupts a fragile supply chain. Gaining the ideal of *right product, right place, right time* can be more a matter of luck than of effective inventory management.

What would happen if large organizations in various industries like pharmaceuticals, CPG, manufacturing, retail, and other industries could apply the power of artificial intelligence and machine learning to solve the previously unsolvable riddles of inventory management? They can. The time to embrace this is now.

Leaders are seizing the opportunity offered through what's called 'cognitive inventory management', referring to the 'thinking' capacity of AI to understand the multitude of real-time dynamics that affect inventory levels. Cognitive inventory management is distinguished from traditional tools in its ability to predict scenarios, recommend actions, and take actions, either with human approval or autonomously. AI-powered cognitive inventory management makes recommendations that address such questions as:

1. How can we reduce working capital in excess stock?
2. What is the best way to get a product from factory to warehouse?
3. How can we best manage expiring inventory?
4. What is our optimal minimum and or maximum safety stock?
5. Why are we always overstocked at one warehouse?

Presented with those questions/recommendations, inventory managers can accept, reject, or revise a recommended action. And once they gain confidence in cognitive inventory management, managers can allow the system to function autonomously, freeing up time from routine tasks to focus on more strategic decision making.

Cognitive inventory management goes far beyond conventional tools and the limited insights they provide. Based in the cloud, it extends the benefits that organizations have already seen by moving applications into a more accessible cloud environment from siloed on-premise systems.

Consider CPG companies that are facing challenges such as product volatility in a given market. It's a constant struggle to try to balance inventory against erratic demand, given hundreds of millions of material movements a day and billions of transactions a year.

For such CPG companies, cognitive inventory management harnesses data from disparate systems, including ERP, CRM, MES, WMS, planning, logistics, weather, data lakes, Excel sheets, etc. It tracks stock in, stock out, and stock remaining, and accounts for such factors as order volatility, demand volatility, production volume, available stock, and more.

Operating artificial intelligence, cognitive inventory management can then recommend optimal stock levels for hundreds or thousands of SKUs at any given distribution center. That's traditionally been the role of human planners, but data volumes and complexity make it virtually impossible for humans to truly optimize inventory management.

Savings can amount to hundreds of millions of dollars as CPG companies avoid tying up working capital, and the high costs of excess inventory consuming valuable warehouse space. CPG companies can also fine-tune production to demand and improve service levels, driving the newfound cost efficiency across the organization.

Hiring more planners and supply chain managers won't solve the problem. Neither will outdated legacy software that relies on statistics. AI offers a tremendously exciting opportunity to at last gain full control over inventory. For companies looking to adopt AI, they should consider very carefully the following points:

Be bold with next-generation technology: companies with innovative leaders who embrace technologies like AI, IoT, and others can make a quantum leap ahead of rivals stuck in the status quo of 1990s-style software and brute-force processes. We're seeing that first-hand as global organizations begin reaping the rewards of cognitive inventory management.

Don't wait; the future is now: it's easy to rationalize putting off an AI project until you upgrade your ERP or deploy a new planning tool. That's an opportunity lost. The beauty of an AI solution is that it layers atop your existing legacy or cloud systems. AI non-invasively complements your infrastructure with groundbreaking capabilities that can forever reshape how you manage inventory.

Take a holistic approach: it's sound practice to first focus AI on a particular issue, such as balancing stock across distribution centers

(DCs), but with a holistic approach that captures data from multiple systems. Since DC stock levels are influenced by dynamics both downstream and upstream of a DC, AI should be applied across all aspects of the supply chain that affect stock levels.

AI-based cognitive automation is still young, but already it's rewriting the rules of inventory management. In a matter of years, the waste and inefficiency of conventional inventory management will no longer be written off as a cost of doing business. Cognitive inventory management gives planners and supply chain leaders capabilities far beyond what's been possible in the past.

2

HOW BIG DATA IS CHANGING INVENTORY MANAGEMENT

The global economy is on the verge of a major upheaval in the way inventory is managed. This transformation is a result of the availability of the huge amounts of real-time data that are now routinely generated on the Internet and through the interconnected world of enterprise software systems and smart products. In order to make effective use of this new data and to stay competitive, managers will need to redesign their supply chain processes.

I am referring about going beyond using traditional historical data on past sales and stock outs. It is now possible to link data generated by all product interactions (including orders, examinations, and reviews by actual and potential customers) and transactions generated by suppliers and competitors who connect via Internet websites and cloud portals. This data can be used by material-management systems to control ordering and distribution of products throughout a company's extended supply chain. In addition, any data that is synchronized with these product interactions can also be accessed and linked.

Advanced machine learning and optimization algorithms – other forms of digitalization – can look for and exploit observed patterns, correlations, and relationships among data basics and supply chain decisions – e.g., when to order a widget, how many widgets to order, where to put them, and so on (*widgets-sounds like accounting 101*). Such algorithms can be trained and tested using past data. They then can be implemented and evaluated for performance vigor based on actual customer demands.

This matters because the traditional archetype for supply chain inventory management is to develop sophisticated tools to generate forecasts that accurately predict the value and the level of uncertainty of future demand. These forecasts are then used as an input to an optimization problem that evaluates tradeoffs and respects constraints in order to come up with decisions about managing materials. This process, which is embodied in all current material-management planning and control systems, can be replaced by a process that looks for the best relationship among all of the data and the decisions. Based on learning from the past, a 'best' relationship can be identified, which is better than the decisions derived from the traditional approach.

The power of computer learning, supplemented by management input based on context-specific knowledge, is used to find the best relationship between all possible decisions and full range of the data. Use of this relationship can lead to better operational performance. It will lead to better outcomes because it utilizes all of the data available to current methods along with extensive additional data that currently is ignored and which may be relevant.

While many challenges remain, it is clear that a new approach that uses all of the data that is becoming available is inevitable, given the connectivity, capacity, and transparency of data sources along with the vast computing power and data storage capacity available at a low cost. Like all planning systems, the proof will be in the results, when intelligent systems based on this approach are applied in practice. Change is coming to the world of inventory management and those that embrace this change will be ahead of the game. Successful adoption of this change will require active involvement of multiple functions within the firm along with a high level of coordination with both upstream and downstream supply chain partners as well as engagement with customers.

In most firms' situations, the volume of data is too big, moves too fast, and exceeds processing capacity of existing applications. Despite these challenges and limitations, big data has the potential to help companies improve operations, increase profitability, and make faster and more intelligent business decisions.

Below are four ways big data is changing the way companies manage inventory:

1. **Improved operational efficiency**: with big data, operations managers may have an overview of real-time operations and better access to metrics, which helps to remove bottlenecks and improve efficiency. Big data enables supply chains to proactively enhance performance compared to traditional models.
2. **Maximized sales and profits**: in the wholesale distribution industry, access to real-time data helps finance directors to manage tight profit margins with greater insights. This ensures that maximum profits can be achieved from investments.
3. **Increased customer service levels**: having access to real-time customer demand pattern data helps service managers match inventory and inventory levels with customer orders accurately, which will contribute to increased customer service levels. Data can be analyzed to predict seasonal trends, spikes, or depressions in customer demand to ensure the right levels of inventory are maintained at all times.
4. **Reduced costs by migrating to the cloud**: a software-as-a-service (SaaS) approach for IT management means that the cloud-based nature of big data reduces hardware and maintenance costs. It can also be seamlessly integrated into existing systems at low costs.

Before looking for a specific solution that supports big data operations, it is highly recommended to have a general checkup of the systems already in place as well as of the implemented processes. In the area of inventory, we identified 12 questions one has to examine and answer to determine how well your business manages inventory. The 12 questions are the following:

1. Are you able to break down your operating inventory into the three major categories when reporting levels – cycle, excess, and obsolete

stock? By understanding the current status of your inventory on hand you can start assessing the root cause of why excess stock, also known as 'over stock', has built up in your warehouses. This analysis will help you take steps towards dealing with obsolete stock levels, as well. Ideally, your business is only carrying cycle stock or 'healthy' inventory items to meet customer demand.

2. What is the current service level or fill rate achieved by each warehouse? Do you know how that KPI is calculated? Clarify the difference between service level and fill rate. Service level is the probability of not having stock outs and fill rate is the fraction of order fulfilled. Both of these KPIs can be calculated in many different ways.

3. Who decides key inventory-related policies such as determining the right balance between customer service and cost-effective product inventory levels? It is important to have company-wide agreement when it comes to balancing target service levels compared to inflating carrying costs. To avoid making decisions within departmental silos, executives with insights into the whole supply chain need to have a major say in the fundamental issues that impact inventory management.

4. How often do you update your demand forecast in your enterprise resource planning (ERP) system? Demand forecasting should work as an active part of your ERP system in order to forecast purchase and stock requirements to predict customer buying habits. Most ERPs are good at placing min/max order quantities, but items being reordered are seldom optimized to keep costs contained. Demand forecasts need to be fine-tuned to ensure inventory levels are optimized while meeting customer demands and keeping costs under control. If demand forecasts are calculated manually, planners need to ensure that it's done on a regular basis for each stock keeping unit (SKU) and that the ERP system is kept up to date for the replenishment calculations. This can be a very labor-intensive job without automation.

5. How accurate are your demand forecasts? Are you able to follow demand trends or the product lifecycle's of items? Are there seasonal factors you need to consider, and how is that managed? Do you apply the best possible forecast technique for different demand

patterns or do you use a simple moving average as a forecasting tool? Do you calculate your forecast accuracy? Understanding and following the lifecycles of your products will help you to better forecast your demand, ensuring you don't miss sales opportunities, and you will have healthier stock levels over time and not end up with excess or obsolete stock in your warehouses. To determine the most suitable forecasting technique the demand patterns need to be identified first. Different forecasting techniques should be applied at different phases of the product lifecycle to best exploit the available historical data and degree of market knowledge. Demand types will vary as a product moves from new entry to fast mover to declining or end of life stages. Forecast error is an important factor that affects the overall performance of your business. Calculating your forecast accuracy at the SKU level will help planners to continue enhancing forecasting process and accuracy.

6. How does your company calculate your safety stock levels? Are you using statistical formulas that incorporate forecast errors, uncertainties in lead times, and service-level data for each SKU? Or are you using a rule of thumb? The ideal way to set your safety stock levels is to calculate them statistically based on what you have learned from previous forecasts. Inventory optimization software that manages the calculation for you is even better. Safety stock should be driven off of your forecast error, target service level, and take supply variabilities into account. If your business is using rule-of-thumb metrics for safety stock, you are likely carrying too much inventory and underperforming on your customer service targets.

7. Do you recalculate safety stock levels on a regular basis to ensure they are up to date? In the ideal world, safety stock-level calculations are made on a monthly basis for every SKU. If it is done manually in a spreadsheet a good target is to review and update your calculations every 3–6 months. Typically, the more time between updates the more risk there is of your excess stock levels piling up.

8. How do you calculate order quantities? How much to order can be based on two criteria: the ordered quantity can be a predetermined fixed order quantity (FOQ). Or a variable quantity, which supplements the inventory in each case up to a certain order level. If you reorder a product at the right time, you will protect customer

service levels. The amount you order, however, will determine your company's profitability over time. Companies with efficient inventory management have processes and systems that continually or perpetually calculate the optimal order quantity based on sound mathematical models. The order quantity for each SKU is automatically updated and tracked in the ERP system for ongoing optimization.

9. How do you determine the optimal frequency for ordering inventory? An order is made either if inventory has fallen below a defined level (reorder point system) or if a predetermined period, fixed order cycle (FOC) system, has expired. When it comes to procurement practices, companies should consider calculations that minimize the overall cost such as inventory and changeover costs.

10. Is your optimal reorder frequency and order quantities reviewed and recalculated on a regular basis as part of a continuous improvement process? Once you have reached your target service level or fill rate, you will have to put new processes in place to continuously reduce your inventory levels while still maintaining your service-level goals.

11. Do you have regular visibility into excess and obsolete stock, and is it linked to targeted action plans to sell off or reduce this inventory? Typically, excess and obsolete stock stems from ineffective demand forecasting, rule-of-thumb methods for deciding safety stock levels and outdated replenishment parameters in the company's ERP system. Inventory planners and managers should establish processes to determine why excesses are being created and then develop a plan of action to sell it off. The fear of the write-off has led to a large buildup over time of obsolete inventory.

12. Do you apply the above practices to all parts of your inventory management, including finished goods, raw material, works in process, and spare parts? The most common mistake made by businesses today is that they are only looking at a small fraction of all inventory being carried. Specifically, multi-echelon supply chains that have large warehouse networks. As a result, they miss potential savings across the entire supply chain, that build up over time

It's important to realize when your organization is in need of an inventory optimization solution. Make no mistake about it, sophisticated inventory management isn't an option anymore; it's a necessity. If you are not able to serve your customers effectively, your organization will not be able to stay competitive or keep up with growing demand. If you struggle with any of the assessment questions, you are likely in need of inventory optimization software to support your current inventory management processes and ERP system. Of course, the software will need to be implemented properly. First we need to discuss the misconceptions of managing inventory in this new age.

3

MISCONCEPTIONS ON MANAGING INVENTORY IN A DIGITAL-DRIVEN WORLD

In this section, we will explore the four common inventory myths that may be costing you money, and examine how to address them with proper inventory management software.

Myth 1 – we can't have stock outs

The importance of being able to fulfill customer orders in a timely fashion is obvious – after all, if you can't they will likely look elsewhere. However, this doesn't mean that you need to carry excessive and costly levels of inventory. Any decent ERP inventory software system will allow you to manage purchasing, taking into account lead times and seasonality, to help forecast demand. Responding to customer demand is an ongoing worry, and as such, it is great to have automated purchasing to reduce this worry.

Myth 2 – if we buy more, we get a much better price

Buying more up front can save you money, but it also comes with substantial cost. Giving up the cash up front for a discount means you could end up in a cash pinch if your cash flow is tight. You will also incur additional carrying costs with extra inventory that you won't likely sell for a while. Here again, forecasting will aid you in determining how much extra inventory you should be willing to take on. If you know, for example, that it will take you two months to sell a large shipment of inventory, perhaps you will consider the discount. If, however, past sales indicate that it will take you 14 months, perhaps the discount just isn't worth it.

Myth 3 – inventory is an asset

Money tied up in inventory cannot be easily accessed – it has to be sold first. Having substantial inventory is not beneficial and serves no direct benefit. Using software to identify dead stock can help you get rid of inventory that's taking up space on shelves which could be better used to temporarily house fast-moving products or for potential new products. Periodic inventory audits or cycle counts can easily be performed with a properly integrated inventory/accounting system to ensure you only put money into the products you are going to sell.

Myth 4 – inventory variety appeals to a variety of customers

Having a variety of products allows you to serve customers across more industries/business types. However, doing so also greatly increases the amount of inventory that you carry. The question is: do you sell enough of these 'other' products to warrant tying up money in your inventory? Specialization is often a better strategy to prevent trying to make everyone happy (hint: it's nearly impossible to make everyone happy and remain profitable). Here again, in-depth reports can aid you in determining which products serve your business the best and allow you to make strategic decisions about your specialization.

Inventory management is knowing what you have in your warehouse and where your stock is located. However, unless it's integrated with your back-office systems, an inventory management system alone can't effectively optimize your inventory, or ensure the inventory asset value on your financial reports matches what is physically in stock – at least not without manual intervention and reconciliation.

To optimize inventory management, leading companies integrate their inventory software directly with back-office and accounting systems. This integration provides a competitive edge with abilities to plan effectively, execute predictably with customers and minimize labor costs and errors associated with manual reconciliation.

Determining the right inventory management system for your business and a strategy for back-office integration requires assessing your needs today and your plans for future growth. To achieve maximum benefits, your integrated solution must be real-time, flexible, transparent to users, reconcilable, and scalable.

The one question I always seem to be asked: why do I need to integrate my inventory management with the back-office system? The first part of the answer is simple – there can no longer be independent silos within an organization's supply chain. All departments are dependent upon a smooth and efficient supply chain. The second part of the answer is a little more complicated.

The three key advantages for a firm to integrate your inventory management software with its accounting and back-office systems are:

- Optimizing inventory to meet product availability and ROI goals
- Providing inventory visibility to supply chain partners
- Stating inventory accurately in financial reports

There are other benefits of integration between inventory and back-office systems, but these three provide the most significant impact to company's profitability. Below are the benefits each will provide to the company.

Inventory optimization: having the right mix and the right amount of inventory on hand is paramount to both customer and investor satisfaction. Customers want 'fresh' product on demand, and investors would prefer no working capital tied up in inventory. Balancing these conflicting objectives is tricky and carrying extra inventory wastes money beyond the initial material and labor investment.

Activities such as storing, counting, and reworking inventory tie up additional working capital, and potentially reduce the availability of products your customers want. Planning the right level and amount of inventory requires your sales order, purchase order, and planning systems to have real-time visibility of your inventory.

Supply chain visibility: many companies are using supply chain partners to manage their inventory levels and customer shipments. To do so effectively, the inventory system must be integrated not only with the company's back-office systems but also with supplier and 3PL, or third-party logistics, systems. By seeing your company's fluctuating inventory levels, suppliers can ensure their product is available at your warehouse or 3PL when your customers need it.

Accurate financial reports: ensuring your annual reports and tax returns are accurate is crucial for your investors and the government. Inventory value can be a significant portion of your stated assets and the recorded value in your books must match the physical value in your warehouse. The only effective way to ensure financial integrity in your company reporting is to integrate the transactions in your inventory system with your back-office chart of accounts.

Inventory and back-office system integration must be real-time, flexible, transparent to users, reconcilable, and scalable. Being real-time provides the best visibility to your customers and supply chain partners, and ensures that your financial reports are always up to date and accurate.

Users want the integration to be flexible and transparent, as continuous changes in business processes may require adjustments to the integration. Users don't want to have to think about the integration; they just want it to work! Scalability is sometimes forgotten about during the integration design, but if neglected, it will come back to haunt you when your company's success overloads it with high transaction volumes.

A prime example of the modern technological advanced inventory management software is NetSuite's cloud-based system – NetSuite Demand Planning software.

Designed to enable wholesalers, manufacturers, retailers, and distributors to achieve best-in-class inventory management practices, NetSuite Demand Planning enables companies to forecast peaks and troughs in demand and minimize capital tied up in inventory. Leveraging NetSuite's integrated business management suite, NetSuite's new demand planning bridges the gap between the front office and back office – allowing companies to tightly align sales forecasts with inventory replenishment plans. This supports businesses with minimizing excess inventory, eliminating stock outs, and improving customer satisfaction. Combined with the ease of deployment of cloud computing and integrated business suite, NetSuite puts the power of completely integrated demand planning into the hands of companies of all sizes and geographical locations.

Businesses can use sales forecasts to build an inventory plan and even augment the plan with special predictions, such as marketing input on new product launches. Alternatively, inventory plans can even be built using statistical forecasting models such as linear regression, moving averages, and seasonal averages, based on historical sales data. As part of a fully integrated supply chain, these projections can even be automatically delivered to upstream providers, ensuring that the entire flow from raw materials to end customers is managed with minimal disruption and optimal inventory levels at each step in the chain.

In today's competitive world, businesses need to run lean in the current economy. Businesses have struggled with legacy-disconnected ERP, inflexible tools, and out-of-date spreadsheets to try and manage demand. The result has meant high IT overhead, and infrequent, inadequate, and out-of-date plans.

Demand planning is essential for all product companies that are trying to effectively manage inventory to maintain a competitive edge in the global business community.

An intelligent demand planning software enables companies to:

- Improve inventory forecast accuracy – by automatically building inventory forecasts from real-time data, businesses can reduce demand planning cycle time, lower risk of error, and operationalize the demand planning process.
- Reduce excess inventory or risk of stock outs – by ensuring the right amount of inventory is kept on hand to effectively meet demand rather than having to tie up unnecessary capital in inventory.
- Minimize manual restock processes – by automating the actual inventory replenishment plan and creating the necessary purchase orders and work orders to meet anticipated demand, NetSuite Demand Planning frees up stakeholders to focus on more strategic activities.

The power of NetSuite Demand Planning or other similar software is in integrating historical and sales forecast data, together with inventory and replenishment processes. An integrated business management suite across front and back office provides the critical foundation for this kind of collaboration and coordination, and when combined with advanced demand planning, businesses gain flexibility, innovation, and a competitive advantage that's hard for competitors to match.

These misconceptions or myths of inventory management are not restricted to manual operations but include inventory software. Inventory management goes hand in hand with inventory software, provided that the software is fully integrated within the entire supply chain. We will now demystify five myths of inventory management software.

Myth 1 – there is no need of software for inventory management

Here's a statement very commonly spoken by enterprises that use old-school methods to manage their inventory. Many companies maintain that they do not need any software solution to manage inventory. Their claim to fame is: 'we can do it on our own by maintaining everything in the books.' By 'book' they are referencing Excel spreadsheets. This is a short-term solution. If the plan is to grow the company thereby increasing inventory by 50%, a spreadsheet becomes too cumbersome to evaluate, reconcile, and maintain. Inventory will be 'lost' if only using this method.

Managing your warehouse with spreadsheets will lead you to manage a big library too along with your inventory. Replacing old books with software is a necessity for proper warehouse management. An inventory management software saves time and resources. It also saves you from keeping local copies. Software stores your data on a centralized system, making it easy for you to save your data and share it with colleagues and vendors. With this system, you can track and search past records with a few clicks.

Myth 2 – inventory management software solutions are not reliable

We rely more upon the human brain and not on computers. We don't believe inventory management software and rely more on human work and manage every single thing ourselves. Everything is registered in the book by our own employees.

The human brain is more powerful than computers, but computers can work 24/7 and more proficiently. An inventory management software works error free and minimizes your workload. Inventory management software systems store data securely and make it easily accessible. New advancement in the technologies like Internet of things, artificial intelligence, and machine learning are driving automation to your warehouse management. They may process your work automatically and do not require much involvement of your workforce. However, software is a tool; albeit a very good one, it is just a tool. It is useless without sound inventory management processes and the training of the staff in these processes to ensure the correct data is recorded onto the software.

Myth 3 – there needs to be a constant check on inventory

This myth stands with enterprises that just started using inventory management software solutions. They think that they should check their inventory frequently with accurate figures. Companies believe they must not fall short of stock, or run over the stock capacity.

When you are using technologically advanced software, there is no need to pay much attention towards the existing stock. There are some good technology-supported warehouse management software that run everything automatically. With the help of analytics, these inventory management solutions manage stock according to the demand and expected supply.

Myth 4 – only inventory specialists can track orders and place demand

There are many stereotyped perceptions about inventory management. One of them is, 'Only an inventory specialist can track your inventory and place orders.'

With so much of technology support, inventory management software solutions can track your inventory in real time and place orders automatically. They store data on a centralized system and create separate barcodes for every single product. With these barcodes, any of your employees can track, manage, and process orders. An inventory management software allows users to see detailed information about any specific order in their system. It also generates the demand and processes the order request for raw material to create further stock.

Myth 5 – my warehouse is too messed up for a software

Some warehouse owners run a very complex process, and they do have a very messy inventory management. They cut this solution off with the misconception, 'my inventory management is too messed up and cannot be handled by a software.'

Technology was created to kill messed-up processes. So, when it comes time to the deal with your warehouse disorder, it not only kills it but also implants efficiency into it. All you have to do is choose the right software for your warehouse management. An efficient installation is also crucial. It syncs all parts of your warehouse and work centrally. This brings coordination in all parts of your enterprise. Also, it shares data centrally with all. So, the decision-making process is fast, clear, and confusion-free.

Building smooth systems to manage your inventory's stock can be a challenge. Whichever industry you are currently working, training is the initial part that you must complete in order to attain the best results. Likewise, for getting the best results from inventory management software, training is the best way to establish effective inventory management.

The challenge of protecting sensitive data has increased exponentially. Companies think that using any technology or inventory management software increases the risk of sensitive data being stolen by their competitors or anyone. However, the inventory management software developers know the importance of data and the concept of data encryption. Data encryption is a relatively easy approach that such software offers for the protection of data, and that is outside the seller's direct control.

These were a few of the myths that industries think about when using inventory management software. Many small companies try to get their business underway and then organize the inventory management later down the track. However, inventory management is the fundamental thing that has to be there when a business launches. Misconceptions and myths about inventory management software can cause contradictory impacts on the business. With the right tool, your business can remain competitive, profitable, and very informed about the trends in the market.

4

BEST PRACTICES IN INVENTORY MANAGEMENT IN THE DIGITAL AGE

Inventory management isn't something many professionals enjoy thinking about, even those who work in the field. That's one of the primary reasons it's helpful to implement best practices that are proven to streamline inventory management processes. Making an otherwise cumbersome, time-consuming, and frustrating process simpler and more efficient will save you many headaches, keep your workforce on-task and business processes flowing, and even boost the company bottom line. Inventory management isn't something that's limited to warehouses. Even manufacturing businesses benefit from sound inventory management for maintenance, repair, and operations equipment.

Are you managing your inventory as effectively as possible? It's OK if you're not. Most businesses have plenty of areas to improve, especially in their warehouses. But if you don't begin the process of upgrading and streamlining your business operations now, you'll easily slip into bad habits, inefficient practices, and a high cost of inventory. By following inventory management best practices, you'll run and manage an efficient and effective business and warehouse year after year.

The following are ten inventory methods and practices that will help you optimize your inventory, whether your business is manufacturing or distribution.

1. Categorize your inventory using ABC analysis

ABC analysis is a technique for arranging your inventory into a hierarchy of most important to least important items.

Here's what an ABC analysis would look like in practice:

- **A-items** are the best-selling, highest priority stock and require regular reordering and constant quality review.
- **B-items** are valuable, medium-priority stock and usually require monthly reordering.
- **C-items** are low-priority stock and are typically carried in high volumes with minimal reordering.

Organizing your stock within your warehouse according to how they sell and how much value they bring your business will help you optimize storage space and streamline order fulfillment.

2. Optimize your pick and pack process

The pick and pack process is a set of procedures and tools that your employees use to fulfill customer orders quickly and efficiently. There are several types of pick and pack methods.

- Discrete order picking
- Batch picking
- Wave picking
- Zone picking

There are five ways to maximize the pick and pack process for effective inventory management:

1. **Design your warehouse for efficiency** by placing your top-selling items nearest the packing station.

2. **Keep your warehouse well-organized** by cleaning every area and removing clutter.
3. **Implement and program a warehouse management system** so that the items picked are listed in the order the picker will find them.
4. **Double check each order for accurate counting**.
5. **Use barcodes or RFIDs** on every piece of inventory for easy counting.

3. Establish your inventory KPIs

Inventory key performance indicators measure your performance in a particular area over a specific amount of time towards a certain goal. They help to eliminate guesswork by giving you clear milestones to hit every week, quarter, or year. With them, you'll have the data you need to make smart, strategic decisions for your business.

Here are six inventory KPIs you should focus on:

1. Inventory carrying costs
2. Inventory write-off and inventory write-down
3. Rate of inventory turnover
4. Cycle time
5. Order status and tracking
6. Fill rate

4. Use batch tracking

Batch tracking is sometimes referred to as lot tracking, and it's a process for efficiently tracing goods along the distribution chain using batch numbers. A 'batch' refers to a particular set of goods that were produced together and which used the same materials. Use an automatic batch tracking system in order to enter information about all the products within your batch – keeping that information at your fingertips if you need to access it quickly, as in the case of a product recall.

5. Use an accurate reorder point formula

A reorder point formula tells you approximately when you should order more stock – when you've reached the lowest amount of inventory you can sustain before you need more. You can stop being a victim of market spikes and slumps by using a proven, mathematical equation to help you consistently order the right amount of stock each month. This equation is called a reorder point formula.

Here's a reorder point formula you can use today:

(Average Daily Unit Sales × Average Lead Time in Days)

    + Safety Stock = Reorder Point

6. Carry safety stock inventory

Safety stock inventory is a small, surplus amount of inventory you keep on hand to guard against variability in market demand and lead times. Without safety stock inventory you could experience:

- Loss of revenue
- Lost customers
- A loss in market share

What makes safety stock a critical inventory management best practice is that you'll reap all these benefits by using it:

- Protection against unexpected spikes in demand
- Prevention of stock outs
- Compensation for inaccurate market forecasts
- A buffer for longer-than-expected lead times

7. Optimize your inventory turnover rates

The rate of inventory turnover is a measurement of the number of times your inventory is sold or used in a given time period, usually per year. By calculating your rate of inventory turnover, you'll have a better grasp on the market demand for your products, on the amount of obsolete stock you may be carrying, and what steps you need to take to sell or stock more inventory – depending on your turnover rate.

This is the simple formula for calculating your inventory turnover rate:

Cost of Goods Sold (COGS)/Average Inventory

The following are four ways to increase your rate of inventory turnover:

1. Experiment with pricing.
2. Liquidate obsolete stock.
3. Forecast customer demand.
4. Redistribute your inventory to other warehouses.

8. Streamline your inventory counting

Streamlining your inventory counting process – the steps you take to count inventory – will help you mitigate the possibility of your staff making costly mistakes. A well-structured stocktaking process will include all the steps required to keep your staff working efficiently to uncover discrepancies and inaccuracies while keeping them engaged and focused.

Here are a couple of ways to streamline your counting:

- Schedule your counts to reduce impact on business operations.
- Clean and organize your stockroom before performing your counts.
- Know what stock you're counting and how you're counting it.
- Open and count absolutely everything – no guesswork allowed.

9. Reduce your inventory

Most businesses have 20–40% of their working capital tied up in inventory – so if you're closer to the 40% end, it's probably time to create an inventory reduction strategy. The goal is to find your inventory sweet spot – where you have the lowest possible inventory levels without being under stocked – in order to maximize growth and profitability for your business.

Here are three inventory reduction methods you can follow:

1. **Lower lead times** by tracking your existing lead times, sharing sales data with your suppliers, and reducing minimum order quantities.
2. **Eliminate obsolete inventory** by reworking or modifying your stock, offering a discount, or dating it for a tax write-off.

3. **Improve inventory forecasting** through real-time tracking and reporting, integrated communication, and large volume inventory management tools.

10. Use a cloud-based inventory management system

One of the best business-changing decisions you can make is to stop using Excel inventory management and start using cloud-based inventory management. Unlike locally installed applications, cloud-based inventory management software allows you to pay for the features you need now and seamlessly upgrade when you need to in the future. You'll pay a single, predictable subscription fee for a 'package' that best suits your particular feature needs and team size; then, upgrading is just a few clicks away when your business growth justifies a more powerful platform. On top of stress-free upgrades, cloud software companies work in the background to make sure things continue to run smoothly, and should you need any questions answered or breaks fixed, they'll have a support team standing by to assist you.

Such a system is not just a best practice. It is also the one tool that ties all the other best practices together. From streamlining your counts to optimizing your inventory turnover rates to batch tracking – a cloud-based inventory management software will help you improve every area of your business operations.

In summation, even with these ten best practices to be followed for efficient inventory management, there are challenges throughout the entire organization which might throw a 'hitch' into accurate inventory control. The ultimate goal of effective inventory management is to balance customer needs while minimizing the carrying costs of excess items. The biggest challenges to more effective inventory management often have to do with conflicting objectives of other departments that need to be involved in inventory decisions and the difficulty of accurately predicting supply and demand. Inventory managers that attempt to bring other departments into the discussions around more effective inventory management often find that each department has its own goals with regard to inventory.

Sales and customer service: concerned with rapid order fulfillment and customer satisfaction – may want higher levels of stock at all times

Procurement: concerned with getting the best per-unit price for an item – might get a better deal on ordering 100 items at a time rather than 10

Finance: concerned with lowering carrying costs – may want minimal stock to be carried on hand

Inventory management: concerned with balancing these differing objectives when developing its inventory management strategies

With regard to supply and demand, some macroeconomic forces may always remain somewhat unpredictable. Unexpected economic downturns, for instance, are hard to predict. However, those forces that can be measured and predicted, such as supplier performance or seasonality of products, must be incorporated into the inventory management process. Closer collaboration with suppliers can help to predict when shortages might occur, while working with sales and marketing to forecast demand can help to ensure that stock levels are optimized to meet changing customer needs.

Part 5

SUPPLY CHAIN WAREHOUSING
IN THE 21ST CENTURY

Warehousing has become a core competency, a strategic weapon that many companies are using to enhance their competitive position. At the same time, the warehouse is undergoing unbelievable challenges that make warehouse excellence harder to achieve. The planning, managing, and improving of today's warehouse operations require a much more professional approach to warehousing than previously adopted.

As a result, e-commerce companies are struggling to make do with what's available in warehouse space, because while all of them may want newly built, up-to-date warehouses with high ceilings, modern amenities, and new-tech compatibility, they can't always find those warehouses in the right location.

Efficient execution of a warehouse management lets an organization to improve its competitive advantage by minimizing labor expenses, enhancing customer service, improving inventory accuracy, increasing flexibility, and responsiveness. A sound warehouse management allows a firm to manage inventory in real time, with data as existing as the latest order, shipment, or receipt, and any movement in between.

The warehousing function is very critical within any supply chain. If the products do not move seamlessly within the supply chain, the business would face serious service-related challenges. Hence, it is necessary to drive the performance of the warehouse through key performance indicators. Further, in a continuous improvement environment, it is essential to benchmark against the industry standards in order to drive improvements.

1

THE 20TH-CENTURY WAREHOUSE IS PASSÉ

Facilities built before 2000 still account for 89% of storage space in the United States, and that's forcing tradeoffs.

The average age of warehouses is now 34 years, rendering them 'increasingly obsolete' for companies seeking new tech-friendly warehouses. As a result, the new age of warehousing – e-commerce companies – are struggling to make do with what's available in warehouse space, because while all of them may want newly built, up-to-date warehouses with high ceilings, modern amenities, and new-tech compatibility, they can't always find those warehouses in the right location.

Old warehouses tend to be in more densely populated areas while the newer ones tend to be farther away from those target markets. Warehouses before the e-commerce boom tend to have lower ceilings, uneven floors, and less square footage – making them less attractive to e-commerce companies looking to maximize space and efficiency.

Choosing a warehouse in 2019 and beyond has become a series of tradeoffs and strategic business decisions. The idea of one size fits all is outdated. There are 'old' style warehouses that are in markets where an e-commerce user may not want to be, or they may serve that market from a regional distribution center that's further out, and they might not have to take advantage of that older space. E-commerce users are going to deal with a whole lot more pain if the warehouse is closer to the market. E-commerce may have to give up warehouse height, dock doors, amenities for employees, and even parking if they choose an older warehouse. Often, depending on the business need, they may not have any other choice.

If an e-commerce company's warehouse is farther from the target market, it may end up being more technologically advanced to accelerate operations and deliver quickly to farther away customers. For example, a distant warehouse might use more automation in its processes to keep operations moving quickly and deliver to customers as quickly as a closer warehouse would.

Every major e-commerce user out there is dealing with some kind of concession. Is this an opportunity or a challenge? It might be an opportunity as there is strong demand in the warehouse arena, because e-commerce users need more space to serve consumers, aka Amazon and their 1-million-square-feet fulfillment centers.

Even though warehouse rentals are at a high and vacancies are at the lowest in quite a while, there's also some imbalance with warehouse demand: e-commerce users really want the new, modern warehouses, so those get snapped up first. If an e-commerce company isn't nimble enough, it could miss a good warehouse opportunity.

When one is researching warehouse demand in the marketplace, one tends to look at net warehouse population, and what I found was that of all the new spaces built over the last two years, that has represented almost the entire market demand. The new warehouse space is dominating the demand in the marketplace and with the ever-growing e-commerce market it does not appear that will be altered.

The new demand in warehouse space and the type of warehouse is leading to tertiary markets: more and more e-commerce companies are moving into more remote areas that are close enough to their target markets so they can build or rent the modern warehouse spaces. The 'creation' of the Inland Empire in southern California and the Lehigh Valley logistics hubs are a direct result of this expansion.

Until the old warehouses grow too old to be safe, e-commerce companies will need to keep making tradeoffs and compromises to reach consumers. But e-commerce is growing to dominate consumer spending, so the wear and tear on old warehouses could give way to a new building spree with modern warehouses in optimal locations.

2

THE WAREHOUSE IN THE 21ST CENTURY

HOW TO KEEP UP WITH DISTRIBUTION CENTER AUTOMATION AND DIGITALIZATION

There's no direct or easy path from an outdated facility to a timeless one. Picture the typical warehouse of 15 years ago: workers rode around on fork trucks and pallet jacks, picking and putting away product by the pallet load, loading trailers one at a time or several at a time. Fast forward to today's DC and you'll likely see significant differences fuelled by the rise of e-commerce, omnichannel fulfillment and the growing trend towards buying fresh food online. The imperative now is speed and accuracy in an extremely competitive retail environment. Failure to meet rapidly increasing customer expectations in this new business framework will mean failure.

Thus inside the DC or in today's vernacular – fulfillment centers – the focus has shifted from regular store-bound orders to individual customer orders. The workers are doing completely different work, and are often toiling alongside robots. Even the internal infrastructure is evolving from static racking to massive automated storage and retrieval systems (AS/RS), and goods-to-person setups that are fed by robots. Automation is everywhere, and everything is moving at light speed. Get it right and you win omnichannel e-commerce.

In the remainder of this chapter we will look at some of the ways warehouse and DC operations are evolving and how to ensure that all your systems are in sync to make the most of new strategies and technologies.

However, the old-school warehouse we described above is not a relic. In fact, it's a distribution model that many retailers still use and have implemented in recently commissioned facilities. But it's not a model that serves omnichannel commerce very well. Retailers and other types of companies are being stretched to respond to the demands of combining online orders with brick-and-mortar operations.

The attempt to fulfill store replenishment orders from the same stock that e-commerce orders are picked from is a very difficult situation. E-commerce orders, in addition to individual item picks, need fast fulfillment, packaging for shipment through parcel post, and delivery to disparate locations. The order of complexity is high and the cost of all those touches can be staggering.

Whether manufacturer, retailer, or service company, all are exploring numerous potential solutions to these challenges, each of which is contributing to the rapid evolution of distribution and fulfillment models. The following are the most current solutions to the success of the 21st-century warehouse: automation, integration, hyper-local fulfillment, hyperactive commerce, pickup in store, dock to dock, and digitalization. Each will be discussed further below.

1. Automation: warehouse robotics suppliers cannot keep up with the demand for their product these days. A couple of factors are playing into the new popularity of warehouse robotics. Human labor is expensive, error prone, and hard to find. Low unemployment rates are making warehouse fulfillment jobs harder and harder to fill. Robots move faster than humans. They can operate 24/7, never unionize, and can be deployed and re-deployed flexibly. A system set up for goods-to-person fulfillment using automation plus humans, for example, would need to have an accurate forecast for ten years out in order to pay off. Robots can also work alongside humans, now, with cobots (collaborative robots) demonstrating they are fully capable of safely picking from the same totes as a

human partner and can roam the fulfillment center floor without running anyone over.

2. Integration: robots and automation at these levels of sophistication require a great deal of coordination. Making the best use of expensive assets like massive self-supporting AS/RS buildings or robotic fulfillment systems means that all the parts of the supply chain feeding into and flowing out of the DC must be carefully orchestrated. With a fully automated building, you don't leave the scheduling of inbound loads to fallible humans with a spreadsheet and telephone or email. That's where a comprehensive, automated transportation management system is needed to ensure trailers arrive at the docks when they are supposed to be there. Likewise, with a large, automated warehouse, it's highly likely that there will be trailers to manage in the yard. These systems take the guesswork and human error out of scheduling and yard management, integrating seamlessly with the automation that powers the DC (ERP). The systems talk to each other, which means your people don't have to spend their time fruitlessly tracking down truck drivers to find out when they plan to arrive, or searching through thousands of trailers in the yard to find the one that's needed now. That's how a relatively small investment in yard management and dock scheduling can help make the most of a big investment in DC technology.

3. Hyper-local: when you think 'distribution center', the image that comes to mind is typically a big box located on the outskirts of a major center, usually close to major transportation arteries. Once again, e-commerce and omnichannel requirements are skewing that picture. Because of the pressure to offer faster fulfillment times or the growing trend of ordering fresh food online, it makes sense to fulfill orders close to the ultimate consumer. Some distributors, like Amazon, have their fulfillment centers no more than 90 miles away from customers. For grocery retailers, the idea is catching on. US grocer Albertsons, powered by artificial intelligence, will take an online order and deliver totes of produce and other goods to a human picker to fulfill customer orders. The retailer says the system will fill orders faster and is scaled to work within the existing retail infrastructure. Other retailers have unveiled similar strategies, some, like Sam's Club turning poorly performing stores into local

DCs, or department stores like Macy's and Nordstrom opening multiple, smaller DCs.

4. Hyperactive commerce: the objective of these strategies is to ensure that online orders are filled as quickly as possible. But with multiplying locations, with smaller inventory holdings and ever-increasing speeds to manage, getting the product into the local DC has never been more important. **If the product is not on the shelf when it's needed for sale, then the customer may be lost forever**. When you only have a limited amount of room for fast-moving items, you need to ensure that the trailer they are on gets to your dock door on time.

5. In-store pick up: while a hyper-local fulfillment strategy can be part of a retailer's strategy, many are continuing to rely on in-store picking to fill e-commerce orders. It takes the pressure off old-school DCs, and turns the store into an order-fulfillment center. Relying on suppliers to ensure that product is on the shelf is a recently resurgent tactic to ensure that inventory is managed to prevent stock outs. In the past this process was called 'vendor-managed inventory' (VMI). Now, it is called 'order-to-shelf'. It is risky and brilliant at the same time because it downloads the day-to-day scheduling of product to the manufacturer or distributor. However, the manufacturer or distributor must ensure stock outs.

6. Dock to dock: typical retail stores don't have a lot of docks to manage increasing volumes of inbound trailers. That means there may be scheduling challenges to accommodate greater numbers of trucks arriving to unload smaller replenishment orders. Every time a customer or picker finds an empty shelf in the store it's lost revenue and lost reputation. By alleviating the pressure on store receiving staff to manage the arrival of numerous trailers, automated dock scheduling allows the inbound truck driver to set his or her own appointment. Staff members will no longer have to track drivers down to find out when they're coming, or worse, divert them when there's no room.

Mobile technology is the backbone that holds it all together. Many of the spectacular advances in supply chain control in recent years have been made possible by the rise of technologies like the Internet of things and cloud computing. With disparate and remote segments of the supply chain communicating and people relying on Internet-connected devices to track and manage inventory, these technologies are crucial elements of success.

Sensor-based inventory control and cloud-based software for omnichannel operations gives you the ability to keep up to date and remain relevant to the next wave of supply chain workers who thrive in this digital environment. Implementing a bring-your-own-devise program for warehouse workers, for example, allows for faster training, lower costs, and a happier workforce. There's always a risk in such programs, and making sure systems stay secure is a huge concern for today's operations managers. Cyber threats are not limited to the potential theft of customers' credit card data. With hyper-connectivity, the whole supply chain could be brought down by a hacker with nefarious intentions.

Distribution centers are displaying a lot of diversity as supply chain operations managers strive to find creative, cost-effective solutions to manage their omnichannel sales. However, from the tiny, hyper-local fulfillment center right up to the giant, lights-out automated DC they all have a couple things in common. First is the need for speed in e-commerce fulfillment, and second, the overwhelming digitization of operational control. These two features combined make the ideal condition to apply digital solutions that ensure connectivity where they will deliver instantly measurable results.

When speed of delivery is of the essence, being able to predict and control stock levels in your facility – be it huge or hyper-local – is a competitive advantage. With the 21st-century warehouse now a reality, you cannot afford to be managing with 20th-century tools.

3

THE FIVE STEPS TO A 21ST-CENTURY WAREHOUSE

In the 20th century, the normal strategy for solving productivity issues in the warehouse or distribution center was to throw bodies at it. However, with an economy spanning from lethargic to moribund along with sky-rocketing costs for labor, fuel, materials, and more, a company ends looking to automate.

But there is more to using automation and/or technology than simply removing human beings and inserting machines. Designing a true 21st-century warehouse, whether a 'green' or a sustainable one or a retrofit, requires a lot of thinking, pre-planning, and testing. The following are five critical dynamics to consider to ensure your new warehouse design delivers the results you want.

Business needs

This may seem obvious at first, but in my experience it's not. It's very easy to go to a trade show or see an article about a piece of equipment and start trying to figure out how to get the CFO to approve the budget item. The problem is too often that this is done without really thinking through why you need that piece of technology and how it fits into the overall business.

It is best to first take a step back and look at how the business operates today using all the business data you have available. Some of the questions that need to be asked are:

- What do you do well?
- Where are your weaknesses?
- If you can only afford a partial automation strategy now, what effect will that have on other areas – both upstream and downstream?
- Will that great piece of automation be idle a significant portion of the time because your manual unloading process can't deliver goods to that area fast enough?
- Will it create a bottleneck further down the process by overloading the next station?

The answers to these questions and more must be taken into consideration before making any automation decisions.

It's also critical to look five years down the road at how the business, and even your industry, might change. Any time you're laying out a warehouse, you're making a significant investment of time, resources, and cash. You want to be sure you're taking into consideration how your business needs could evolve. A prime example is the goods-to-person (GTP) technology. Today, you may not be selling to individual consumers and thus can afford to focus on case quantities and above. But if your competition is already starting to offer GTP capabilities, you may have to as well to stay competitive. You need to have the flexibility in your operation to quickly make that change. It also helps to look at predictions of what general business conditions will be like in a few years. Rising fuel costs can have a different effect on business needs compared to a rapid economic recovery. Be sure you take the time to think through the possible scenarios before committing to a single direction. Flexibility can be expensive, and therefore, it is imperative that the design team systematically evaluates and matches the appropriate levels of flexibility with the forecasted business requirements.

Building blocks

After you've determined the business needs today and in the near future, start looking at the building blocks of the system. You will want to know what you need to accomplish in the warehouse space, and all the steps in the process. You don't need to get specific yet. It's more important to look at what the overall flow should be, which is based on the business data you accumulated through the questions you answered in the first step.

You'll probably have an idea of the technologies you plan to install. So then it's a matter of how those technologies or building blocks can be used most effectively based on your business needs. You might want to see if an automated storage and retrieval system can be used not only as a workflow buffer into packing but also for residual handling and to drive the picking process. The objective at this point is to get those building blocks down on paper and then start looking at the different ways you can use them.

You may not get to one final design at this point. In fact, you may have several. You'll then need to start weighing the viability of each design concept based on factors such as the economics – initial capital outlay and the cost to operate that system – the use of space within the warehouse and how the various technologies fit together. In the last case, you may find that the individual technologies you've selected are all good, but don't flow together into a single system the way they should. This is the time to discover all of that, before you start determining your final design.

Simulation

Once you have the right design, it's time for simulation. This is a very important step, though some try to move too quickly through this phase or pass over it entirely in a desire to get the new facility up and running. One of the big reasons running simulations is critical is that the technology used today requires more initial capital outlay than simply hiring humans to do the work. Simulation helps you mitigate risk and validates your design concept as the further you go the more expensive errors become.

A good simulation lets you plug the data you have into the design you've created to see how well the system achieves the stated goals. It then allows you to try different scenarios to see how the system reacts – including testing to see how quickly it recovers from a disaster. By building a working model of the system, you can ensure you have the opportunity to fully evaluate and validate it to remove doubt about whether the system is viable for your needs. If one or more pieces don't work as planned, or the design isn't delivering the results you need to achieve, this is the time to find out – before you've invested a great deal of time and money to put it in place.

During simulation, it is essential to begin establishing the requirements for the system controls and software. Incorporating the actual system controls approach in the model should be part of the simulation. One residual effect of having a full working model in place is it can be used to train new personnel later. Secondly, if business conditions change in a year or two, you can plug new technologies, system rates, or other data into the existing simulation to see the effects they will have.

Integration

Once you're satisfied with the results of the simulation, it's time to move into the working layout of the facility. This is where warehouse design ceases to be theoretical and starts becoming practical. Rather than saying you want a sorter here or an AS/RS there, it's time to select the specific technologies and their configuration.

As you are moving into real-time warehousing, you will need to involve engineering teams at this point – mezzanine or structural, mechanical, and electrical groups. Real-life warehouses are rarely as simple and pristine as we would like. There are always obstacles to work around, such as a sprinkler system pipe or a support beam in an inconvenient position, as well as traffic flow and other issues to be considered. You will also need to determine the electrical power, communications, and HVAC requirements. You want to allow for all of that in this planning phase since, again, it is less costly to make adjustments on paper than it is in the field. You want to ensure you're using the space you have most effectively and efficiently.

Maximizing the value of your investment in warehouse design isn't just about the physical space; it's also about making sure controls are properly integrated to make it easy for personnel to operate a relatively complex system. When you apply all the different software packages, they must work as a single cohesive system, instead of a mish-mash of unrelated applications.

While it seems self-evident, it's not as easy as it sounds. The software for most material handling equipment is designed to be self-contained. Integrating all of the controls together usually takes much longer than most organizations expect. But this customization is critical for delivering the results you seek.

Implementation and training

The final phase – implementation and training – involves taking all the hard work and due diligence planning and translating it into an actual warehouse or distribution center. At this point you will be procuring equipment, finalizing the software coding, testing, and ensuring everything works the way it should.

While the importance of this phase should not be minimized, by following the first four steps properly there shouldn't be a lot of need for adjustment now. Almost all the kinks should be worked out, allowing you to move quickly through this phase and start realizing the return on investment. You'll also want to start training your personnel on the new system so they're familiar with the equipment and procedures and can hit the ground running the day you cut the ribbon.

When warehouses were primarily dependent on human beings, there was far more room for error and adjustment in warehouse design. After all, no mechanism is more flexible than people. With today's emphasis on automation and efficiency, however, that is no longer the case. You have to get it right the first time.

Perform the due diligence to be sure the design is right for your business needs and that everyone, including the maintenance staff, is fully trained on the system and know how to get the most out of it. It may seem like a lot of work at first, but it's the fast track to a successful 21st-century warehouse design.

Part 6

SUPPLY CHAIN AND THE
NEW DEMAND PLANNING

While it may seem surprising, the discipline of the supply chain is only 30+ years old. Like many important ideas, it grew out of a simple but powerful observation. While departments like sourcing, manufacturing, and transportation were working cooperatively, their interactions lacked the discipline of process and structure. Missing from this scenario was a department called planning.

Even now the same precision and discipline which gave birth to the supply chain is lacking in the demand planning or forecasting side of most businesses. Think about what your company spends on marketing, advertising, promotion, and sales. Then add the costs and complexity of managing customer relationships and you come to a compelling opportunity.

What if you could bring the discipline and precision of process, structure, and metrics to the demand side of your business in the same way you use them on the supply side of your business? And, what if the results continuously increased revenues, margins, and profits? Well, some of America's most successful companies have answered these questions and found powerful and enviable results.

The new business model for the 21st century is a combination of the demand chain and the supply chain. Why? Because the demand chain puts revenues and profits into your business, while the supply chain takes costs and complexities out of your business. The combination creates a continuous growth, competitively advantaged, and high-performance company.

1

TEN CRITICAL DIFFERENCES BETWEEN THE CENTURIES IN DEMAND PLANNING

In a time of great uncertainty and unprecedented change, business, institutions, and charities are vying for a way to move forward. That change can only come from a complete understanding of the way people are thinking and acting in their working lives. It is all new, so you need a different type of knowledge to deal with it.

In the blink of an eye we find ourselves at the beginning of the third decade of the 21st century, a lifetime away from a world we left 20 years ago. Whether you are a private business, a public company, or a charity or not for profit, you are facing the realization that your old business model is no longer enough. It may still work, but barely. Here are ten points that all organizations must now take into account when making decisions.

1. The 21st century is as far away from the 20th century as the 20th was from the Dark Ages.
2. The people who put you out of business in the 21st century may not be your competitors.
3. The transition from Global 2.0 to Global 3.0 is going to be difficult for many businesses without a guide.

4. The role of customer satisfaction may be secondary to survival in a declining market.
5. The four pillars of the 20th-century business model.
6. Without a social license, all the political support in the world may not be enough to get your project over the line.
7. Economic and political communities no longer need to operate in a physical space once a critical level of economic sustainability is reached.
8. The social good or 'commons' is going to be tested increasingly in the next five years – not only as it relates to business but also to religious and social institutions, government, and media.
9. We may experience two worlds in the Global 3.0 era.
10. The biggest barrier to fundraising for new ventures and expansions is and will continue to be the inability to monetize risk.

Perhaps a better way of understanding this drastic change is with these two tables:

In the 20th century, no matter the type of organization, if you had the right product at the right price and spent enough on marketing and distribution, then your chances of success were high.

That model no longer works! Distribution has changed dramatically and marketing is far more fragmented and broader based. The public sector is becoming increasingly intrusive into business, and the public has become more responsive to the actions of all organizations, whether not for profit, religious, corporate, or government.

Without a thorough understanding of where the community stands, your projections will not be a reliable reflection of what may happen. Product development and customer satisfaction is unlikely to save a project when the bulk of the community who are not even customers or your constituency are against you. The challenge is how to turn this around to achieve a positive outcome for all stakeholders.

2

DEMAND PLANNING NEEDS TO INCORPORATE MORE THAN ...

Demand management needs to incorporate more than just planning and fulfillment. There is a big need today for companies to strengthen their demand management capabilities. Supply chain executives consistently cite demand volatility and the lack of demand visibility as two of their top challenges. Additionally, innovation and growth depend on a company's ability to quickly and effectively process and respond to demand.

The solution is to move beyond thinking of demand management in the traditional terms of supply and demand planning and fulfillment. Instead, companies need to create a comprehensive demand management strategy that also encompasses demand forecasting, sensing, and shaping. Thus, this five-stage best-practice methodology was created for demand strategy.

Demand forecasting: organizations with a strong demand forecasting process do not just look at historical sales activity. They also incorporate more forward-looking signals, such as sales forecasts or marketing plans, and downstream demand data, such as retail point of sale or channel sales data. This data, however, is often incomplete. Gartner says that tools such as pattern recognition and machine learning can help predict missing data values.

Demand planning: companies can improve their demand planning process by increasing the frequency of forecasts, which will lead to using more accurate and timely data. Prior to deciding on a consensus demand plan, members of sales and operations planning (S&OP) teams should assess multiple forecasts. Mature demand planning processes will also provide models for segmented channels.

Demand sensing: real-time 'sensing' of demand has replaced demand forecasts that are based on rules, particularly in the business-to-consumer world. Demand sensing is also making inroads in the industrial business-to-business realm as companies seek to gain better visibility of demand through indirect wholesale and distribution channels. Demand sensing technologies are now evolving to include simulation and optimization techniques, which can help companies with mid-term planning.

Demand shaping: demand shaping includes programs and capabilities such as price management, new product launches, and promotions to increase demand or profitability for products and services. Best practices involve synchronizing supply strategies with demand and product management decisions through processes like S&OP.

Demand fulfillment: companies are increasingly realizing that they need to differentiate their demand fulfillment processes to serve different combinations of products, customers, and channels. For example, certain defined segments or combinations may require a make-to-stock or make-to-forecast model, while others will be configure-to-order or make-to-order.

Almost every company has these five demand management capabilities somewhere in their organization, but they are often scattered across multiple teams and roles. To become better at demand management, companies need to create a structure that connects these abilities to create a well-thought-out response to customer demand.

As a number of these are relatively new capabilities they need to be discussed in further detail.

Demand forecasting: companies must lay aside outdated mass marketing practices. Relying on single assortment, standard pricing and a single 'average location' forecast will not satisfy the 21st-century consumer. With so many factors impacting consumer behavior and increased pressure on profit margins, companies must focus on better understanding the demand for merchandise throughout the buyer's journey. Forecasting predicts and meets consumer demands while controlling pricing and inventory. This is critical because warehousing excess inventory adds overhead costs while under-stocking leads to loss in revenue. Anticipating future consumer actions can be done by evaluating past revenue, deciphering sales patterns, and analyzing buying behavior. The objective is to better manage order quantities, stock and shipment allocation at the store, and SKU levels. By improving demand forecasting, retailers will experience fewer stock outs, improved margins, and more solid overall business results.

Many organizations still are using manual ordering and even resort to relying on their 'gut' reactions when replenishing stock and preparing for promotions. They are relying on last year's shipment-withdrawal data or spreadsheets like Excel to aid in their demand planning. The best business context for demand forecasting is technology and its ability to go beyond inventory replenishment to include planning and collaborative elements. Team members across organizations – from category managers, buyers, managers, and vendors – should be able to reconcile their forecasts using the same system.

Demand planning: recent technological advancements have caused a seismic shift in how individuals interact with businesses. The expectation that consumers should receive instant, cost-effective, and personalized experiences is here to stay, and companies will rise and fall on their ability to scale their operations accordingly.

Nimbleness is, therefore, the name of the game, with companies needing to seize opportunities to engage customers and then immediately deliver on their promises. Given that the latter is highly dependent on a company's particular S&OP processes, make sure your company is poised for success by employing a frictionless (and connected) planning strategy – that is, one that efficiently links your demand planning process to all departments and business objectives, and one that is sensitive to even the slightest changes in demand. So let's assess how to plan for a successful demand planning strategy.

- Overall strategic objectives – forecasting and demand planning shouldn't exist in a vacuum. Clearly define what you're forecasting for, the level of detail desired, the consumer profiles you're targeting, and the reasons for looking at demand in this way. Your demand planners will then be able to make business decisions, such as which forecasting methods to use or how to prioritize orders in the event of an inventory stock out that support your specific goals. In some cases, technology is there to assist in making the best choice.
- Communication and collaboration among people along the supply chain – ensure all the key stakeholders are connected to each other. A common platform where all involved can communicate and collaborate eliminates confusion and reduces the risks with passing Excel spreadsheets or other files back and forth via email. Everyone is kept in the loop with minimal effort.
- Data collection in real time – centralized, accessible, and useful to all parties. If you have a steady, up-to-date flow of data that is kept in one place, accessible to all, and can be easily analyzed – regardless of the file type – you know you're well on your way to achieving a connected planning strategy. By implementing a software solution that enables this kind of data collection process, you can ensure that key stakeholders are all working with the same information.
- Data analysis – while historical data is important when calculating a strong statistical baseline forecast, demand planning should also have an eye towards the future, with no one assuming that past behavior dictates future outcomes. Real-time information such as weather patterns should be considered when making business decisions.

Demand sensing: in this ever-changing and highly connected world, how we adapt to rapid change is the new $10,000 pyramid question at the core of almost every commercial strategy. For supply chain planners, this demands a new level of performance to meet 21st-century consumer expectations.

The most elusive and important change in supply chain management will be the ability to predict the future accurately – predictive demand. Traditional planning and forecasting techniques are slow, unresponsive, relatively inaccurate, and based on legacy technology whose days are numbered.

3

21ST-CENTURY LEADERSHIP VERSUS 20TH-CENTURY LEADERSHIP

It's easy to think that concepts like leadership never really change much from generation to generation, but it couldn't be further from the truth. Leadership styles reflect cultural norms, and a lot has changed in the last 20 years. In the 21st century, leadership has evolved as technology has taken over many aspects of our lives. To be effective in the modern workplace, leaders need to understand how to adapt to new leadership styles. Here's how leadership has changed during the 21st century.

During the 20th century, domineering leadership was often the norm in most organizations. In such a system, management makes all the decisions, and takes very little input from employees on the floor. Decisions are made based on the manager's views and experiences, and they have complete control of the group. Today, workplaces tend to be more collaborative instead of authoritarian, making this style of leadership start to fall out of favor.

While the core qualities that make for great leaders stay the same, there is more flexibility in the accepted leadership styles of today's organizations.

Young companies are more open, accepting, and results-oriented than ever, allowing leaders to use their creativity in order to succeed. There are several emerging styles of leadership that can work in different situations, including:

- Democratic/participative: input from team members is valued and used in decision making
- Transformational/inspirational: leadership inspires team members to find internal motivation to reach specific goals
- Transactional: leadership provides rewards for certain accomplishments

Though these are very different leadership styles, they are often combined to account for different teams' unique qualities. Leaders are starting to become more aware of how differences in employees' personalities and learning styles affect how they respond to leadership. Good leaders are emotionally intelligent and can pick up on cues from others to inform their approach to working with individuals.

There's absolutely no doubt that the mercurial rise of the Internet has affected the way leaders manage their teams. Many employees work from home, and managing remote employees requires even more adaptability and constant communication. Technology affects everything, from the way employees communicate with one another to the evaluation tools available to leaders. Technology can make leadership easier in some ways, but managers must use it well, or it can make leadership disjointed and ineffective. Some managers use technology to avoid contact with employees, completely the opposite of what is needed of a 21st-century leader.

Leaders in every type of industry are acknowledging that it pays to be open and transparent with employees about how the company, the team, and the individual are doing. Today's leaders are generally more empowered to be transparent – inspiring a more engaged and productive workforce. Leaders get out there among the team and give them the information they need to succeed.

As part of the move away from oppressive leadership, more leaders are finding success in leading through inspiration over rigid direction. Of course, leaders do still provide direction, but there is much more trust involved in modern leadership, allowing employees to become inspired to find internal motivation and enjoy unprecedented autonomy.

Leaders still need to help their teams when necessary, and keep employees accountable, but many leaders are finding that allowing employees the room to figure out problems on their own can yield better results than micromanagement.

Leadership will continue to evolve over time, as business practices and cultural values change. Leaders need to be prepared for rapid change, and stay adaptable in order to succeed in modern leadership.

Part 7

SUPPLY CHAIN IN THE AGE OF CUSTOMER SERVICE

Customer service has an ever-increasing role to play in the supply chain. It is responsible for the way customers feel about the product and the company who is selling it, plus customer loyalty plays a part. Customer service today has metamorphosed into a concept deeply related to the way business is done and the profit it generates. The entire idea around companies having kind people responding to customers' inquiries and welcoming them to retail stores has become a myth and largely disappeared.

It is very likely that most of us have had to deal with a company's representative on the phone. We have had to wait for an eternity, not only for our inquiries to be solved but even to speak to a real human being. In addition, we all have had to struggle to understand the rep's accent – because their native language isn't English – and it is very probable that while talking with the rep the background noise was so loud that we couldn't hear the rep's answer. This model, based on companies outsourcing customer service to save some money, goes against customer retention in the supply chain.

1

CONTEMPLATING ON THE HISTORY OF CUSTOMER SERVICE

We have all experienced that feeling of satisfaction after an excellent, seamless customer service transaction where our needs have been met and our expectations exceeded. In today's business environment, achieving that is a complex process. Depending on the product or service, the best in customer support will include a combination of assistance in planning, purchasing, delivery, installation, training, troubleshooting, maintenance, upgrading, disposal, and proper handling should something go wrong. It is not a new idea; for as long as there have been products to sell in a competitive environment, there has been a need for good service to attract and retain customers.

Some of the first documented examples of customer service emerged as early as the mid-1800s. In 1868, Watkins Liniment offered the first-ever unconditional money-back guarantee, unheard of in those days. The offer, while generous, meant that the customer may have to endure a full day on horseback to return the item to the store, however. Another customer service milestone occurred in 1889 in Italy when the royal family received the first door-to-door hot pizza delivery from Raffaele Esposito, Naples's most famous pizza chef. Restaurant delivery may be commonplace now, but at that time, it was novel for companies to make a priority of serving their customers where and when they want.

The single most important transformation in customer service came in 1876 with Alexander Graham Bell's invention of the telephone. The telephone introduced a new means to contact local businesses which until then required personal contact.

By 1894, with the invention of the switchboard and the completion of the transcontinental railway, customers in need of service could directly contact stores and businesses across the country to make requests, gather information, place orders, arrange for delivery, or register complaints. For over 50 years this was the norm for customer service, until the second half of the 20th century.

With the 1960s came the advent of PABX or Private Automated Business Exchanges, allowing for the growth of 'call centers' (a term coined in 1983). Forward-thinking companies began filling large rooms with agents whose sole purpose was to answer and resolve customer issues on the spot. By 1967, call centers were further enhanced by AT&T's introduction of the toll free 1-800 number. Soon, call centers began using interactive voice response (IVR) technology, which allowed consumers to voice a limited number of commands, such as 'yes' or 'representative', further streamlining the calling process.

Since the 1990s, the Internet has completely reframed how customers receive support from a company. Whether through websites, email, instant message, one-to-one chat, or social media outlets such as Facebook or Twitter, consumers can get information, make purchases, leave messages, arrange appointments, make payments, register complaints, find answers, or arrange for returns any time of the day or night.

The latest technologies, such as video chat, surveys, mobile applications, RFID, and location-based information, continue to transform how businesses meet customers' needs and have raised the bar in terms of their expectations. Today's customer support needs to be available in a variety of ways through numerous channels. Innovative companies like Amazon are leading the way; customers can access Amazon on a laptop, phone, or tablet, and easily search for an item, gather information, make a purchase, arrange for fast delivery, view historical transactions, add credit cards connected to the account, edit shipping and billing addresses, arrange for returns, review a product, and view the status of all past and present orders. Now, Amazon is looking into same-day delivery through the use of local delivery services and, in the future, possibly through the use of drones.

Achieving this level of excellence in service and support starts with a clear understanding of what customers want. CRM (Customer relationship management) software developed in the 1990s, was the first technology to help businesses track and analyze customer behavior. With the acquisition of this data, companies began rewarding gifts such as cash back on credit cards, frequent-flier miles, and discounts for multiple purchases to repeat customers. Now, more sophisticated, cloud-based CRM solutions from companies like Salesforce.com and others provide an abundance of customer behavioral analytics to help businesses pinpoint the specific services their customers need in a timely and efficient manner.

2

CUSTOMER SERVICE
RE-INVENTED FOR THE 21ST
CENTURY

In this new age of customer service, there are those who argue that canned 'scripts' are the direct opposite of great service. Customer service should be a conversation instead of a cold, formal, and lifeless play on words.

So, one could ask, how is customer service and supply chain intertwined? With customer service the aspiration is to stand out from the crowd – surpass the competition and become indispensable.

This is where flexible responses can be quite useful. These responses allow the customer service representatives to have an idea of what to say to customers but also allow for flexibility to adapt and add their own personality to the conversation.

The idea of customer service can be quite reassuring for those companies whose goal is to create an excellent customer service experience. This works provided a firm understands one crucial element: standard customer service practice is not right for every customer.

Customer service best practices need to be tailored to each customer's precise needs or situation. Let's have a little fun now. Below are several customer service practices that will most certainly drive customers and potential customers right into the arms of your competition:

1. Failure to hire employees with the correct persona. Not everyone is cut out to work face-to-face with the customer. There are five words that help define the modern customer service department – sincerity, understanding, care, cooperation, and cheerfulness.
2. The thought process that customer service training is 'one day and over'. Yes, a strong orientation training process is important, but a company needs to commit to ongoing customer service training.
3. The failure to devote the time, effort, and flexibility to see the situation from the customer's point of view. For instance, park where the customer's park, use the customer entrance, telephone on the customer service line, and use the same e-commerce website customers engage in. Do this and you will learn about any company problem as opposed to reading the reviews on Yelp.
4. The language barrier. It could mean two things – require a translator or language miscues. Verbal communication needs to be gentle, kind, and brand suitable, never showing your back to a customer.
5. Failure to be realistic with time. It includes being insensitive to your customer's perception of time. Bear in mind this customer service motto: a perfect product, delivered late, is a defect.
6. Meaning of money. Money means different things to each customer. Money can mean different things to the same customer, depending on the situation. A firm must adjust its way of thinking of money to match the particular customer's version of money.
7. Discrimination through channels. This includes gift cards that only work on the website, items that cannot be returned via UPS or FedEx but only by the customer going to the brick-and-mortar storefront.
8. Not realizing that customer service and your company's reputation starts before they engage on your website or come to the establishment.

To combat these poor customer service practices, good systems need to be in place. Below you will find a few examples of these good systems that will engage your customers as opposed to losing them:

1. If you don't know the answers say so. But say so like this, 'Great question. Let me find out for you right now.'
2. If an item is not available, saying the item is unavailable at this time does not solve the customer situation or put them at ease that all is being done to meet their needs. Instead, this is the context I would use – the product won't be available till next month, but I can place the order for you now and ensure it is sent to you as soon as it arrives at our facility.
3. Having received a defective product is very disconcerting to a customer. Even more so is how the situation is handled. This is where understanding, care, and cheerfulness come into play. Explain that there was a slight mistake in the manufacturing process or it was damaged in the shipping process and then offer to send a brand new product out to the customer immediately.

No doubt it is hard to arrive at a solid customer service process or processes. Even when you think it is accomplished and things were handled flawlessly, some people simply do not want to be conciliatory.

But never, never let this stop you from putting forth the best effort.

3

HOW WILL CUSTOMER SERVICE BE REINVENTED FOR THE DIGITAL AGE?

As the digital age advances further into the 21st century – with the continuing surge of e-commerce now making up a total of 17% of all retail sales in the United States – it is not just retailers that need to put their focus on improving their supply chains in order to win and retain business.

As people and companies have more information at their fingertips than ever before, customer expectations are growing and changing. Today's consumer is fickle, price sensitive, and at the same time, demanding a high-quality experience. Companies have to carefully navigate change, anticipate a range of consumer futures, and stress test all their assumptions.

In a globalized world, where climate change and human rights issues are everyone's business, there is a greater spotlight on ethical sourcing and environmental sustainability. In this context, organizations must work harder than ever to maintain their social license to operate and encourage ethical behaviors across their extended supply chain networks.

Traditional methods of manufacturing goods and moving them from place to place no longer work in a digital age. Companies need to evolve their supply chain strategies to deliver against the demands that omnichannel (any time, any place) requires of the consumer value chain.

Today, we are seeing large multi-national organizations with little supply chain visibility, which leaves them unable to meet customer demands and exposes them to more risk. There are inventory levels that are askew, high operating costs, not to mention low customer satisfaction and service levels.

Today, supply chain reinvention is not something restricted to manufacturing or logistics. Instead, the entire customer journey is at the heart of the process – which means everyone in the business must be involved in reinventing how the operation supports the growth of the business.

The need of growth demands that companies keep doing what they do best, while also looking at the long term – and focusing their future not so much on what their competitors are doing but at how their customers' expectations are evolving.

Manufacturers in the consumer products industry have always been close to the customer to observe how people use and interact with their products, but in recent years, one of the leading players has accelerated their process of product development further. Using leading-edge technology, big data, and behavioral science, and by cultivating an innovation culture, the manufacturer is able to better understand customers' behaviors and the contexts that shape those behaviors.

Is your organization ready for supply chain customer service reinvention? If so, these three questions must still be asked and answered.

1. **Identification**: how easily can I identify the areas of our supply chain that cause the biggest challenges for our business?
2. **Information**: how do we harness the power of our own data and tap into insights from suppliers and customers to understand how our supply chain is performing?
3. **Integration**: is advanced technology, such as AI and blockchain, integrating into our supply chain to optimize end-to-end performance?

4

IMPROVING CUSTOMER SERVICE IN THE AGE OF E-COMMERCE

With the ever-growing e-commerce market, manufacturers are not the only industry that needs to revamp their entire customer service culture, mission, and vision. Retailers of all types, shapes, and sizes are being pushed to put their focus on improving their supply chains in order to win and retain business.

Retailers used to be able to lean on the stability of brick-and-mortar stores to provide a satisfactory customer experience. When a customer walked into a physical store, they knew exactly what to expect and were rewarded with instant gratification and the ability to take their purchases home the same day. Since the rise of the digital age, technology is shaping how customers purchase from retailers, and the customer experience is fundamentally different online.

Customer experience is defined as 'the customer's perceptions and related feelings caused by the one-off and cumulative effect of interactions with a supplier's employees, channels, systems and products.'

At a brick-and-mortar store, a retailer maintains control of the overall shopping experience by training staff, creating a pleasing shopping environment, and streamlining the check-out process. But that is changing fast. With a digital 'store front', retailers can only influence their customers' experience through friendly or easy-to-use enhancements and supply chain improvements.

Digital shoppers are demanding more from their e-commerce platforms:

Flexibility – customers want the ability to choose the service type they need. Choosing the mode helps customers customize their experience.

Speed – getting product quickly and when desired is becoming more important as *2-day delivery* becomes standard. Designating when the product will arrive helps customers plan ahead and allows them to be more self-sufficient. (*As I write this Amazon is trying to alter the landscape with 24-hour delivery.*)

Tracking – customers everywhere are demanding tracking capabilities. In order for customers to have confidence that their product has shipped and will arrive on time, a standard tracking feature needs to be implemented.

Alerts – in addition to tracking capabilities, up-to-date alerts keep customers' expectations realistic when unforeseen events take place in the supply chain. Customers appreciate alerts to weather delays and other interruptions so that they can react proactively to late deliveries.

Today's connected consumers demand both choice and flexibility when it comes to receiving their online orders – and will not hesitate to move loyalty if they encounter unsatisfactory delivery options. In order to keep customers coming back, customer focus, a customer-first attitude, and navigating internal politics of change must become the mentality of the company.

5

CUSTOMER-FOCUS INNOVATION

Ignore this at the peril of your business.

Bluntly, we are in the age of the customer! While the customer is not always right, he always has the right to choose. Customer focus and a customer-focused approach to building customers into advocates is perhaps your most important task. It all starts with listening to your customers. A firm must ask the following three questions:

1. Do you know who your most important customers are?
2. Do you know who your influencers are?
3. Do you know why they come back to do business with you?

These are important questions whose answers provide valuable insights for your business.

Just as companies are learning to engage their employees, it is just as important to engage customers. Customers remember and value personal experiences that demonstrate deep understanding and respect for their needs. There is a fine line between a bad, a good, and a great customer experience.

You need to know your customers and understand what keeps them up at night in order to build great customer experiences. Great customer experiences are the foundation for great customer service, both are essential for building advocates and influencers.

Businesses need to take their customer service to the next level. The best approaches are by being more responsive and proactive, delivering on their promises, and listening and observing to gain insights and then acting on them.

The ability for a business to serve its customers in a responsive way that is consistent with meeting or beating their expectations will prove to be the ultimate differentiator separating the winners from the losers.

6

CUSTOMER-FIRST CULTURE
AND ALIGNMENT

In today's competitive market place there can be few organizations that do not desire to be customer focused, and even fewer that do not recognize how important employees are in delivering this. The bad news is that still few are truly succeeding in creating a customer-focus culture where the customer is king. This focus upon the impact of the employee in building a customer culture is becoming a key issue for those who want to maintain a competitive advantage.

In this chapter we will investigate the reasons for the gap between realization of converting customer strategy to culture and delivering against it to create a customer-oriented culture.

Most organizations have vision and or mission statements. However, few if any organizations:

1. Base their values on customer feedback
2. Involve their employees in the development of values
3. Link these values to their brand

4. Encourage their employees to align their behaviors to the values
5. Reward their employees for 'living the brand'

As a consequence, organizational values such as 'honesty', 'teamwork, 'partnering', and 'creativity' although espoused by businesses, become no more than empty words: meaningless to both the customer and the employee. If this is the case, how can a company build culture change around customers?

Organizations such as Virgin, Nike, and the US retailer Nordstrom, have succeeded in creating strong brands with powerful brand promises. Through listening to customer needs and via consultation with employees, they have been able to identify brand values which form the backbone of how they do business with the customer and how employees are managed – in short they create a customer-focus culture that realizes the customer vision.

They believe that the 'customer is king' concept starts at the top of the organization. Employees look to the top team to model the desired behaviors in all areas and in creating a customer-focus culture no less. The author has worked with many boards who have encouraged employees to 'live the brand'. Yet their own behavior has been far from consistent with the desired brand values. Little wonder that the values are not adopted on a widespread basis and converting customer strategy to customer culture remains a pipe dream.

Organizations such as Barclays and AT&T have developed leadership behaviors and employee competencies which directly reflect brand values. These in turn are linked to customer needs and are surely the only way to ensure that culture change around customers is successful.

Members of top teams need to regularly assess to what extent their behaviors in relation to customer culture are aligned to the brand and the commitment to the customer vision. They need to also encourage this process across the organization if a truly customer-oriented culture is to emerge.

Many organizations do not place enough value on the insight their employees have into their customers' needs. Whether this is based upon day-to-day interactions or more formal business reviews, this is an invaluable resource that should be fully utilized before contacting customers to gather their views as it will provide an excellent framework of knowledge on which to build. This is a key stage of ensuring employee engagement to help deliver a positive customer experience.

Many companies today, particularly in the service sector, carry out some form of customer satisfaction measurement. When it comes to budget setting, the vast majority of organizations approve the budget for asking their customers for feedback on how they perceive the organization's performance. However, very few companies develop budgets around what should be done as a result of the survey findings. It is this 'lack of resources' that prevents the vast majority of companies from successfully implementing countermeasures based upon customer feedback and is the major reason for the lack of service improvements and building culture change around customers.

This problem is caused not by a lack of desire by companies to improve things for customers, but by a lack of alignment between a desire to listen to customers and their organization's customer-oriented culture. Although many companies do have a strategic vision of being 'customer focused', they struggle to implement this through functional strategies such as the marketing and customer care strategies, leading to a failure to implement a genuine customer culture.

One of the trends over recent years has been to believe that the implementation of a customer relationship management (CRM) system will deliver the corporate vision in relation to building a customer culture. Yet many CRM systems have failed to deliver – why?

Findings on the progress of CRM programs include:

- CRM is a fantasy in most organizations. Over 60% of CRM projects end in some form of failure.
- 80% of all CRM initiatives fail and provide no reasonable ROI.
- More than 90% of meta clients are examining the financial justifications for CRM. Many are taking a step back.

Fundamentally, CRM is a software package that will manipulate data to provide one view of the customer and further guidance on how to:

- Segment the customers
- Target the customers
- Package the products to the customers

- Sell their customer base
- Bill the customers

CRM does have some success with this, but the crucial element that gets overlooked with CRM is that on its own it does not help you understand your customer needs or build a customer culture. It is always about what you as a supplier can do to your customers, and not what you can do with or for your customers. To be customer focused and to develop culture change around customers, you need to work in partnership with your customers and allow them to opt into the relationship. Once customers have opted in, trust and cooperation can be developed, which in turn brings mutual benefits. In addition, for CRM to be successful, employees need to 'buy-in' to the process and want to make it work. Again, a high degree of trust and cooperation are required here too if you want to be truly customer oriented.

To further align the business with customer needs, companies are increasingly using a tool called customer journey mapping (very similar to value stream mapping in Lean Six Sigma). This helps identify the journey that the customer takes through an organization, often transferring from one organizational silo to another. If the business is to become customer oriented the use of customer journey mapping is key to understand your customers' experience from their viewpoint rather than examining it by internal organizational silo.

So how do you gain customers' and employees' trust and build a customer-oriented culture? You have to start by looking at what are the key elements of any relationship, and these are true for both the customer-supplier and the employee-employer relationship:

- Accessibility
- Responsiveness
- Keeping the public informed
- Knowledgeable people
- Promptness
- Keeping promises
- Follow up
- No surprises
- Doing it right the first time

This list essentially provides a checklist for any customer or employee satisfaction measurement, as only when you are performing well against these will your customer/employee start to trust the relationship. The actual words of the questionnaire would be developed around talking to both employees and customers to ensure that the questions are phrased in a way that is meaningful to the customer and actionable by the company.

So what are companies doing today? Companies are gaining customer feedback; it is what happens after that data has been collected where the real challenges start.

The first problem area seems to be the communication of findings to employees – an essential aspect if the company is to achieve its ambition of converting customer strategy to customer culture. After all, it is these employees that will be delivering the countermeasures against issues raised by customers. The author has found that companies often recognize they have problems to resolve with the customer, but they score relatively poorly on how well they communicate and develop improvement plans to both their customers and their employees. It appears that once a poor communicator, companies are sadly consistent in this aspect of their business, no matter who the audience are, customer or employee.

This poor communication of customer feedback results in individual employees not understanding how it impacts their roles and responsibilities, which in turn limits their ability to drive any change within the company and their desire to 'live the brand' and create a customer-oriented culture.

The inevitable conclusion to this lack of communication leading to lack of activity is that all parties will not perceive any value in providing feedback, and instead will simply look to build relationships with other parties. Solving the problems ascertained from the analysis of customer feedback and acting upon the feedback is crucial.

In order for this gap to be closed and a customer-oriented culture to prevail, work needs to be done on translating customer feedback into the context of desired behaviors. This has to be looked at from the point of view of all the parties, i.e. company, customer, and employee:

In too many companies, listening to customers is taken as an annual event, with this single snapshot of customers' views being taken as the definitive view of the customer. Ironically, this point is often made when the answers received do not match up with expectations, and the research is seen as having 'taken place at the wrong time', but strangely this is never raised when the findings exceed expectations!

Customer feedback, whether external or internal, is a continuous event in a customer-oriented culture. The annual customer or employee satisfaction measurement programs may be taken as providing some of the headlines, but it is more regular feedback that will not only provide the detail behind the headlines but also provide evidence of the impact of any countermeasures that have been deployed.

As well as communicating the feedback of customer and employee surveys, senior management need to ensure that service providers are involved in the resolution of customer issues. This can be encouraged via the use of service improvement teams and action groups. Often, training and coaching interventions need to be designed to support desired behaviors and create a culture where the customer is king. Organizations such as BUPA have successfully developed leadership programs, supported by 360 findings, to allow individuals to refine and test customer-value-based leadership behaviors. They have also included all employees in brand awareness workshops with the intention of allowing employees to see how their behavior impacts on the customer and delivering a customer-oriented service.

In order to sustain a customer focus, organizations need to ensure that customer and employee feedback is regular and that brand values are in line with customer and employee needs. One organization with whom I worked recently found that its customer values and desired employee behaviors that had been developed five years ago needed to be revisited and updated in the light of customer and employee feedback. The benefit of clear customer-oriented values and behaviors and regular feedback is that it provides a framework against which employers can:

- Recruit new staff
- Measure performance
- Plan career development
- Reward customer-oriented behavior

Ultimately, the effectiveness of this approach in converting customer strategy to customer culture can be evaluated via such measures as the balanced scorecard, increases in the number of loyal customers, profitability, and growth. The key performance indicators for changing customer cultures are 20 questions, yes 20, all of which must be accounted for:

1. Does your management team meet with customers at least once a month (even when there isn't a problem)?
2. Does customer service appear at least once a month on the top team's agenda?
3. Does the management team give equal weighting to customer data as they do to financial data?
4. Do you have a formal customer satisfaction measurement program?
5. Does the customer satisfaction measurement program involve regular, monthly feedback from customers?
6. Are the customer feedback and employee feedback programs aligned?
7. Are your organization's values based on customer and employee feedback?
8. Have behavior codes and competencies been developed based on values?
9. Do individuals receive 360-degree feedback on how well their behaviors are aligned to the brand?
10. Do all employees have a good understanding of how their job provides added value to the customer?
11. Do individuals receive encouragement from their manager to 'live the brand'?
12. Do all employees have a good understanding of what the current customer concerns are?
13. Are service providers involved in service improvement planning and implementation?
14. Do all employees have a good understanding of what is being done to remove customers' concerns?
15. Do employees sometime act as customers, to experience for themselves what it is like to be a customer of theirs?
16. Are training interventions in place to increase customer awareness and align people's behavior to the brand?
17. Are employees selected for their customer orientation?
18. Are employees rewarded upon customer feedback and service orientation? (This can be non-materialistic recognition as well as financial.)

19. Is the balanced score card used to measure customer orientation and performance?
20. Is there a clear link between customer satisfaction, employee satisfaction, and profitability?

7

NAVIGATING THE INTERNAL POLITICS OF CHANGE

In today's fast-paced economy, leaders know that their organization's success may be tightly linked to its ability to change and change again – and again. Most executives have a portfolio of tools that they use for developing their strategic plans, structure, metrics, and other 'hard aspects' of change. However, their approach to tackling the 'softer side of change' and, more specifically, navigating the politics and emotions associated with change, is often more unstructured.

Yet left unattended, skepticism, fear, and panic can wreak havoc on any change process. These types of feelings can create resistance, disengagement, distraction, and burnout. Innovative ideas may get suffocated, time and energy wasted, and change goals sacrificed to short-term self-interest. Performance may also drop as exasperated high-performing employees leave for greener pastures.

There is a five-step process first introduced by MITSLOAN that is designed to enable change leaders to successfully navigate the politics and emotions of change by identifying and leveraging the expertise, skills, and resources of sponsors and promoters; drawing in fence-sitters; learning from positive skeptics; and addressing the concerns of negative skeptics. These five steps are discussed below.

Step 1: Map the political landscape

In every change, politics emerge as stakeholders jockey to represent their interests. Sometimes, stakeholder groups are based on function, product, geographic region, or level. At other times, the political alignments are based on tenure, personal beliefs about what's best for the company, or social demographics.

The first step in working with the emotional and political dimensions of change is for the change leaders to map the political landscape – the key external and internal, formal, and informal stakeholders who will be affected. For a customer service change initiative, the key external stakeholders might include suppliers, customers, communities, government entities, etc. Formal internal stakeholder groups tend to follow the organization chart. In a customer service initiative, they might include people at different levels as well as functional and product divisions or geographic regions.

Step 2: Identify the key influencers within each stakeholder group

Once the key stakeholder groups are mapped, change leaders should identify the key influencers within each group – those individuals who might be able to line up resources, enroll others, build legitimacy and momentum, and provide ideas crucial to driving the change. Influencers are the key individuals who have the resources, skills, or social networks needed to win over the hearts and minds of the larger group.

Most of us are likely already familiar with the idea of targeting key influencers in external word-of-mouth marketing campaigns. However, we may not have applied that concept within our organizations or thought to identify the key influencers in the change initiatives we lead. These power players are just as critical internally because of their ability to energize or derail change. Influencers can either create a positive buzz that helps inspire others in the organization to make the change or, through negative comments, heighten their resistance.

To find key influencers, revisit the organizational map to identify those 'go-to' people whose opinions can sway others. Some might persuade through formal power, such as a top-ranking executive who is looked up to and trusted by many. Others' pull may stem from their expertise, such as an indispensable IT specialist. It is important to spend time up-front identifying these key influencers, listening to their ideas and engaging their participation, because they play a critical role in providing resources, enlisting others, and casting the change in a positive or negative light.

Step 3: Assess influencers' receptiveness to change

Everyone reacts differently to change. Some may be eager, enthusiastic, excited, and hopeful. Others may be confused, angry, or uncertain. However, for the purposes of categorizing receptiveness to change, I have found it helpful to recast and further divide the dispersal curve into six segments: sponsors, promoters, indifferent fence-sitters, cautious fence-sitters, positive skeptics, and negative skeptics.

Sponsors and promoters are the most receptive to change. They welcome change and are easily convinced of its merits. Sponsors are particularly helpful for underscoring the benefits to the customer or the organization, or for offering resources and lending support. Promoters, in contrast, can create optimistic buzz and help to build passion and confidence around change. Bringing both of these types of early adopters on board in the initial phases of change and asking for their support, ideas, input, and commitment can be extremely beneficial in moving change forward, as they have the power to magnify the positive word of mouth.

At the other extreme, influential skeptics tend to fall into two categories. Positive skeptics resist a change because they genuinely believe it has flaws that need to be addressed. These folks are critical to involve and listen to because they offer a reality check on the proposed changes and implementation. They can be a catalyst for useful rethinking of different aspects and often can help uncover snags and complications that could cause trouble or create a backlash. Negative skeptics tend to resist change for more personal and emotional reasons. Often these people are struggling with underlying fears and anxieties about how the change will impact them personally. Working through their concerns is an important part of keeping the change process smooth.

In the middle – and in the majority – are the fence-sitters. They also tend to fall into two groups. The members in the first group are cautious. They watch and wait and are often concerned about the political consequences of moving too fast. They tend to look to their peers for direction or postpone action until most people are on board with the change. Indifferent fence-sitters constitute the other category of the middle majority. Their lack of interest might stem from feeling overcommitted or from a sense that the change is outside their direct scope of responsibility or is not integrated directly into their performance metrics. Addressing the concerns of skeptics early can prevent negative emotions from swaying the cautious or indifferent fence-sitters towards resistance. However, in our experience, it tends to be the energy of influential promoters and sponsors that wins over this fence-sitting majority.

Step 4: Mobilize influential sponsors and promoters

Sponsors and promoters are change champions vital to success, because they have the insight, passion, and energy to aid in the creation of the content, culture, and momentum required for change. They have the social networks to broadcast the change, the acumen to make a compelling case for change, the resources to get things done and the power needed to gain the necessary support to achieve success. Sponsors and promoters bring different sets of strengths and tools to the process that can be critical in converting the middle majority into true believers.

Sponsors have access to financial and human resources and can capture the attention of the C-suite. They can win over key stakeholders. Sponsors are likely to be story shapers who have an ability to connect the change to the strategic vision of the company and its value proposition.

In our customer service initiative, an influential sponsor might be a senior vice president who led the organization through tough challenges in the past and who believes that the new initiative is essential for translating the talk about customer service into practice. Such an executive might be able to work behind the scenes to pull in powerful peers who are fence-sitters or broadcast the strategic rationale and value proposition for customer service at meetings.

Promoters, on the other hand, have connections with a broad range of people throughout the organization. Promoters are story sharers, translating strategy into divisional or region-specific narratives in ways that can be more easily understood. They also cultivate shared ownership for the change by customizing its benefits with respect to a particular function or unit and encourage their colleagues to contribute their own ideas for driving the implementation forward.

In our customer service initiative example, a boundary-spanning promoter from the European division might see the customer service initiative as an opportunity to increase her visibility in the organization. She may be delighted to expand her role as an educator within the organization by sharing best practices and helping with the training and mentoring of groups in other regions. Her connections across the organization, experience working on previous sustainability initiatives in her region, and clear support for the new initiative may also draw in the cautious fence-sitters.

Step 5: Engage influential positive and negative skeptics

Skeptics can either offer tremendous value to a change process or turn a minor hurdle into a major roadblock. Although change leaders may often believe that the concerns of skeptics will naturally dissolve, working with skeptics early in the process is time well invested.

Positive skeptics may offer important perspectives and insights about the vulnerabilities of proposed changes. For example, positive skeptics in the sustainability initiative may include production floor stewards who have heard rumors that an environmental overhaul of their processing plant is in the works but no one has yet communicated the specifics. They may grow resentful that no one is soliciting their input. Bringing them into the process by asking for their ideas and exploring their underlying reasons for opposition invariably will uncover challenges and risks that are better dealt with preemptively. Better yet, a representative from this stakeholder group could be asked to help shape the initiative from the start.

Equally important is working directly with influential negative skeptics. Sometimes consciously, sometimes unwittingly, these cynics may kindle underground resistance that could derail the change if their concerns are not addressed. Returning to the customer service example, many baby-boomer employees might fear they lack the skills needed to succeed in the new environment. They may worry that they will be replaced by younger employees trained to work with the newer, environmentally friendly technologies and processes. Being transparent and up-front about the consequences of the changes, and delineating what opportunities will exist for training and/or outplacement support and exit packages if there are layoffs, would help alleviate some of the anxiety.

Positive or negative, skeptics should be embraced and their concerns heard. Developing action steps to address issues raised by positive skeptics early is important in order to prevent resistance from escalating. Listening carefully to the concerns of negative skeptics is also critical. Addressing their concerns honestly sends a clear message that their perspective is important, that the change will not be force-fed to them and that transparency and openness are valued. This will not only promote success in this change but also build receptivity for future changes that are inevitably around the corner.

If leaders do not have time to address skeptics' concerns directly, they may choose to recruit influential sponsors and promoters to help. However, they should ensure that two-way communication channels are in place. This will ensure that shortcomings of the change highlighted by positive skeptics are not overlooked and will contribute to strategies that alleviate some of the anxieties of negative skeptics.

With globalization, rapid technological change, ever-shifting economic and political conditions, competition from around the world, and short-lived competitive advantage, many companies face a constant need to change, and every change creates a different set of political responses and emotional reactions. While the five-step process outlined here offers a systematic approach for working through these 'softer' dynamics, this approach must be tailored for each specific change initiative.

Business leaders cannot afford to ignore the politics and emotions that arise with change. The five-step process offered here provides leaders with an action-oriented and easy-to-navigate approach for working with the political and emotional dynamics that can either thwart their best-laid plans or drive an important transformation. As sponsors and promoters take on change leadership roles, positive skeptics channel their input and negative skeptics acquire the skills and support to confront their fears constructively, these seemingly unpredictable aspects of change can be leveraged effectively. What's more, they can even ignite a collective passion that will enable the organization to thrive.

Part 8

SUPPLY CHAIN AND PREDICTIVE ANALYSIS

Predictive analytics are increasingly important to supply chain management, making the process more accurate, reliable, and achievable at a reduced cost. To be at the top of your game as a supply chain manager, you need to understand and utilize advanced predictive analytics.

As a large continuous process the supply chain has been extensively studied and is pretty well understood. It goes in well-recognized steps from:

- Procurement
- Inbound logistics
- Parts inventory
- Manufacturing
- Finished goods inventory
- Fulfillment (customer's order to delivery)
- Outbound logistics

While these seven elements of the supply chain are each the focus of separate management activity, visibility over the entire supply chain is also a requirement, particularly visibility into unexpected events in the plan that might mean failure or delay.

For quite a long time, business intelligence (BI) and its historical perspective served quite well. For example, using historical data we could determine that a part takes on average X days to arrive and even calculate standard deviations to make some fairly sophisticated adjustments in our procurement plan. Likewise on the demand side, we could look at historical demand data and try to determine future demand, procurement needs, and production requirements.

Increasingly, there is a requirement to better foresee the future, anticipate future events, and make optimal tradeoffs based on strategic choices of top management. To be at the top of the game in supply chain management now – enter *predictive analytics*.

1

LOOKING INTO THE FUTURE

PREDICTIVE ANALYTICS AND SUPPLY CHAIN

Predictive analytics are increasingly important to supply chain management, making the process more accurate, reliable, and achievable at a reduced cost. To be at the top of your game as a supply chain manager, you need to understand and utilize advanced predictive analytics.

As a large continuous process the supply chain has been extensively studied and is pretty well understood. It goes in well-recognized steps from:

1. Procurement
2. Inbound logistics
3. Parts inventory
4. Manufacturing
5. Finished goods inventory
6. Fulfillment (customer's order to delivery)
7. Outbound logistics

As you can see, these are not completely unique processes. Fulfillment, for example, could easily be understood to encompass all of finished goods inventory, order-to-deliver, and outbound logistics. Manufacturing is understood by some to include all the process steps leading up to that point. But however you divide it, there is agreement that it is one continuous process and that a delay or failure at any point will ripple through the system and prevent efficient execution.

While these seven elements of the supply chain are each the focus of separate management activity, visibility over the entire supply chain is also a requirement, particularly visibility into exceptions to the plan that might mean failure or delay. Historically, 'visibility' has been the key word, along with 'integration'.

Increasingly, a requirement of integration is the ability to better foresee the future, anticipate future events, and make optimal tradeoffs based on intentional strategic choices of top management. In short, to being at the top of the game in supply chain management now requires advanced **predictive analytics**.

From a predictive analytics perspective, about 90% of the problem is forecasting, starting with the demand forecast and letting that trickle back through the process to procurement and logistics planning.

There are long-term forecasts that are more like broad risk assessments to try to evaluate whether our customers will continue to want our product. There is also the downwards view of this same question: are our suppliers sufficiently stable to be able to continue to provide critical resources that we need?

Of course the secret to good forecasting is to keep doing it over and over until you get it right. Forecasts should be continuously updated and incorporate time frames that may be several years out, mid-term forecasts that drive our financial investments in plants and new products, and near-term forecasts that drive actual production and procurement.

If you've spent time in data science, the one thing that should jump out at you is that across all the uses of data science, probably 80% of those have to do with predicting or influencing human behavior. What's unique about supply chain analytics is its dependence on forecasting models.

So where modern predictive analytics begins to make inroads into supply chain management is typically in providing more accurate forecasts. This means testing any of a dozen mathematical forecasting models from

ARIMA through dynamic multiple regression modeling to see which ones work best. There's no pre-existing roadmap here, just test, retest, and finally select a champion method.

The other role for predictive analytics is contributing the mathematics of optimization. Optimization isn't new, but any time there are two or more cost-benefit curves to compare, optimization techniques should be able to suggest the optimum tradeoff between the two, guided by whatever external business conditions you want to impose.

We want the models we create to be easily understood by workers at all levels. Visual displays like dashboards on tablets are increasingly a valuable medium for converting the large-scale action into the specific tasks and needs of the person using it.

This means drilling down to the minuscule level of activities, inventory, procurement, shipping units, and customer orders. Big data architectures are clearly a plus, but even more so the new **hybrid transactions analytic platforms.** These new platforms are completely in-memory, hold 'big data' volumes of data, and remarkably can process both transactional and analytic queries simultaneously. These new tools mean near zero delay in interpreting the inflow of customer orders, current inventory positions, and any manufacturing or external delays into near instantaneous updates to supply chains forecasts and plans at all levels of detail.

Following is a list of activities that could be improved with the application of predictive analytics:

1. **Demand analytics – how is my forecast tracking with actual sales?**

   - Detailed demand forecasting at the level of point of sale (store level, retailer, distribution channel roll-up, etc.)
   - Deviation analysis of forecast versus actual at the SKU level
   - Forecast integration with promotional events and holidays to fine-tune the forecast

Impacts: forecast accuracy, in-store availability, lost sales

2. **Finished inventory optimization – what stock should I hold and where should I position it?**

- Inventory budget optimization
- Safety stock level recommendations
- Segment inventory for tailored and customized fulfillment strategies by customer type

Impacts: inventory cost, customer service levels

3. **Replenishment planning analytics – what, when, and where should I ship?**

- Integrated planning at the retailer, distributor, and channel level
- Optimize fulfillment logistics to account for handling, storage, or warehouse constraints

Impacts: in-store availability, customer service levels

4. **Network planning and optimization – do I have the right network of manufacturing and warehousing facilities?**

- Number of physical plants for manufacture and warehouse
- Optimized flow paths to fulfill different segments of customer demand at the lowest total cost

Impacts: fixed and variable costs of operations

5. **Transportation analytics – optimizing transportation routes and loads including contract compliance**

- Optimizing routes including backhaul
- Optimizing shipment schedules
- Maintaining compliance with transportation contracts

Impacts: freight costs, equipment utilization, contract compliance

6. **Procurement analytics – how to achieve lowest landed cost and secure long-term high-quality supplier partners**

- Scoring models for vendor quality, cost, and stability

While the factory floor is often not considered part of the supply chain – it should be – delays here can obviously impact the overall supply chain performance. At least one technique from predictive analytics is achieving wide acceptance and that is predictive maintenance.

In short, predictive maintenance utilizes different types of sensors on critical, capital-intensive production machinery to detect breakdowns before they occur. The data is initially analyzed by data scientists to prepare predictive models of different failure conditions. Those predictive models are then used to evaluate the incoming streaming data from the equipment, and if a potential fault is detected, depending on the type, a message can be sent to the operator and maintenance staff, or an action can be created to immediately shutdown the machine to avoid damaging the capital asset and further disrupting production.

Supply chain improvements need to happen from both the bottom up and from the top down. Tackling one problem at a time, the bottom-up approach, captures near-term value. But the supply chain should also be a topic for strategic top-down evaluation that's guided by overall business goals. The data and insight that predictive analytics provides for both perspectives lets you address some of the really difficult questions with greater accuracy.

- How fast will the supply chain recover from external shocks?
- How do I plan for those external shocks and protect against them?
- Where are the biggest opportunities for additional profits from the supply chain?
- How can you protect margins when demand falls?
- How can you plan to protect profitability at the product level if a major supplier fails?

To be at the top of your game as a supply chain manager today, you need to understand and utilize advanced predictive analytics.

Now that we have seen how predictive analytics is vital for the future of the supply chain, I will break it down further into several of supply chain disciplines – manufacturing, transportation/logistics and customer service.

2

PREDICTIVE ANALYTICS AND MANUFACTURING

Due to the growth of predictive analytics, manufacturers can vastly improve their operations. They can realize the benefits of increased quality control and supply chain management, plus the cost and time advantages of preventive maintenance. And they are able to improve their product design process thanks to regenerative design. Thusly, this chapter will be broken down into three segments – how predictive analytics is improving manufacturing, how to use predictive analytics in manufacturing, and the four benefits of predictive analytics in manufacturing.

How predictive analytics is improving manufacturing

Increasingly, artificial intelligence predictive analytics is transforming the way the manufacturing industry operates. Its impact is being felt not just by the employees who work on factory floors but also by the executives in the organization's C-suites.

AI predictive analytics is ushering in a new era of smart manufacturing, thanks to the junction of an array of digital technologies such as low-cost sensors, advanced robotics, high-speed networks, real-time analytics, and embedded systems. This new age of futuristic factories has been termed Industry 4.0 as it's the fourth major disruption in modern manufacturing.

Through predictive analytics here are three ways manufacturers are revolutionizing their production processes – quality control, predictive maintenance, and supply chain optimization.

Large factories routinely employ hundreds or thousands of workers to spot defects in products, even in very small parts. An AI-powered machine equipped with a highly sensitive camera can spot the same defects as well as microscopic ones that are not visible to the human eye. Using machine learning, these machine-vision tools are trained on a small set of samples and learn from what they observe. When the machine-vision tools notice a defect or problem, they send an alert. They can detect variations in raw materials, changes in machine behavior, and deviations from recipes, all of which help improve quality control. These increases in quality control translate into more efficient day-to-day operations. This in turn leads to fewer product returns and ultimately improvement in customer satisfaction and brand image.

Unplanned maintenance costs faced by manufacturers amount to an estimated $50 billion each year. Asset failure is responsible for 42% of this unwanted downtime. Now, thanks to commodity sensors, and AI predictive analytics, smart machines can produce real-time reports on their performance, enabling factory staff to perform proactive maintenance before a part, machine, or system falls into disrepair.

As a result, smart manufacturers can save valuable time and resources, especially labor costs and costs to repair or even replace mission-critical equipment. Plus, keeping your equipment properly maintained means you avoid potentially disruptive, and costly, downtime.

AI analytics is improving how manufacturers manage their supply chain operations, from the factory floor to the trucks that deliver the goods, by making the entire process more seamless and efficient.

On a strategic level, AI predictive analytics is enabling executives to better understand the many factors that affect their supply chain and adjust their business operations accordingly. AI algorithms can help the C-suite develop data-based estimates of market demand by analyzing patterns that involve consumer behavior, socioeconomic factors, weather trends, political stability, and more.

As a result, manufacturers can adjust their staffing, inventory, and supply of raw materials to realize unprecedented levels of efficiency.

How to use predictive analytics in manufacturing

Predictive manufacturing systems allow users transparency in operations. The basis of a predictive manufacturing system is the smart software, which is used to control predictive modeling functionalities.

Predictive analytics is the analysis of incoming data to identify problems in advance. Many companies don't have predictive analytics in place, and don't intend to do so in the near future.

Manufacturers are interested in quality control, and making sure that the whole factory is functioning at the best possible efficiency. With predictive analytics, it's possible to improve manufacturing quality and anticipate needs throughout the factory.

The early implementation of mass production was congested with numerous causes of waste, such as overproduction, idle time, logistics, inventory, and unnecessary motion. In the early 1970s, the key edict was to reduce production costs by minimizing and ultimately avoiding the sources of waste. This eventually developed into lean principles and Six Sigma techniques.

The computer age saw the beginning of automation and the flexibility of equipment, such as industrial robots. With these capabilities, manufacturers could establish mass customization or flexible manufacturing and supply consumers with the products they want.

The last two decades saw the unprecedented growth in the improvement and adoption of information technology. This led to the creation of reconfigurable manufacturing, wherein a factory structure can be easily modified so that production capacity can scale up rapidly.

Predictive manufacturing systems allow users transparency in operations. The basis of a predictive manufacturing system is the smart software, which is used to control predictive replication tasks. This gives manufacturers the opportunity to proactively implement mitigating solutions to prevent efficiency loss in manufacturing operations. Predicting equipment performance and the estimation of the time to failure will reduce the effects of these uncertainties.

Predictive analytics will be further involved in everyday manufacturing operations, making the workplace more efficient and safer due to the digitalization of assets, known as digital manufacturing, which allow for digital design and even distributed manufacturing. Manufacturers will be able to enhance their inventory position because of the information garnered by the supply chain and operations. Logistics and transportation managers will have reports on how to reduce transportation costs, which is a heavy percentage of the expense budget.

Predictive analytics provides a predictive probability for each customer, employee, product SKU, component, machine, or other organizational unit to determine, inform, or influence organizational processes that pertain across large numbers of individuals, such as in marketing, credit risk assessment, fraud detection, manufacturing, healthcare, and government operations including law enforcement.

The four benefits of predictive analytics in manufacturing

Predictive analytics is expansive. Some companies astound their customers with recommendations using predictive analytics. Others astound their shareholders with cost reductions derived from predictive analytic models. Manufacturing is no different. Rarely, though, are there high-profile stories about predictive analytics. Industry trade associations talk about the benefits of predictive analytics, but manufacturing-related stories hardly ever get mainstream press coverage.

Individual manufacturers are making predictive analytics work for them. Often, the analytical process is specific to that company's products and processes. The specific insight is not usually directly applicable to other companies, but a few broad areas of predictive analytics are applicable to most manufacturers.

Quality improvement: it is what most people think of first when thinking about predictive analytics in manufacturing. Indeed, formalized statistical analysis has been used in some form of quality control for almost 100 years. Improvements in databases and data storage and easier-to-use analytical software are the big changes for quality improvement. Standard quality improvement analysis is being pushed towards less technical analysts using new software that automates much of the analytical process. Storing more information about products and the manufacturing process also leads to analysis of more factors that influence quality.

Demand: manufacturers need to sell their products. Many times, demand is cyclical or seasonal. In such cases, knowing the peaks, valleys, and short-term changes in demand drives resource allocation in manufacturing. Again, this is nothing new to manufacturing, but predictive analytics allows manufacturers to consider many more factors than they could before. Previously, a demand forecast was simply the best guess of the vice president of sales as to what products would sell. That person's assistant would aggregate the sales forecasts from all the sales reps and then apply a fudge factor – not too scientific.

Predictive analytics takes historical sales data and applies forms of regression to predict future sales based upon past sales. Good predictive analytics modelers find additional factors that influenced sales in the past and apply those factors into forecasted sales models.

Machine utilization: manufacturing engineers spend much of their time maximizing the value of equipment in the factory. Predictive analytics helps with this endeavor as it does with quality improvement, by automating much of the previously performed analysis. Machine utilization combines demand forecast with resources on the manufacturing floor to achieve an optimal schedule. In the past, analytics were often spreadsheet based and subject to substantial assumptions from the person who created the spreadsheet.

Predictive analytics applications for machine scheduling combine forecast for demand with product mix to optimize machine utilization. Using new predictive analytics techniques improves accuracy. In reality, that may only increase the utilization for many machines by a few percentage points, but that still looks good to the finance people when it comes time to buy new production equipment.

3

PREDICTIVE ANALYTICS AND THE TRANSPORTATION MANAGEMENT SYSTEM

There is an unprecedented amount of information available in the transportation industry, which contains immense potential for deriving insights that aid in planning and managing transportation networks. This data is captured from various sources such as onboard sensors and data collection points introduced by passenger counting systems, systems scheduling, asset management systems, ticketing and fare collection systems, and vehicle location systems. Players in the transportation industry can leverage advanced analytical techniques such as predictive analytics to use the available data to improve operations, reduce costs, and better serve travelers.

Any technology that can improve efficiency on a 'more is less' model has the capability of making things much easier for both transit agencies and the passengers they serve. Predictive analytics can fill that role to some degree. With the help of predictive analytics, transportation companies can answer the question of 'What's the best possible outcome?', instead of explaining prior history. In this manner, it can help them with many different capacities, from vehicle fleet maintenance to planning new lines of services. Let us explore some of the critical areas in which predictive analytics will help the transportation industry players:

- Predictive analytics can help companies to **determine the impact of unplanned events** such as a transit labor strike on transportation utilization and the local economy.
- Transit agencies can also understand how subway line closures, planned road-works, or transit maintenance projects can affect public transport. They can then use this insight to **plan the optimum change in transit schedules** and communication strategy to deal with the impact.
- Occurrence of **routine unplanned service incidents** like a traffic accident or vehicle breakdown can be identified and predicted, and optimum responses can be suggested.
- Predictive analytics can **model the impact of various proposed urban development projects to transportation** and help in the identification or alteration of the projects to achieve sustainability objectives while supporting the need for mobility.
- Companies in the transportation industry can **pinpoint events such as bus breakdowns, late-arriving buses, or signal outages** that have the highest economic impact to a transit agency and recommend ways to eliminate the events or reduce the effect.
- Predictive analytics can help transportation players to predict the **impact of the planned expansion of transportation networks** by having a clear understanding of the patterns of usage.
- Transportation agencies can understand when the vehicles require maintenance well in advance with the help of predictive analytics. Such advanced analytics capabilities help to identify irregularities and forecast a range of asset performance risks before trouble arises in the case of vehicles owned by the transportation agency.
- With the help of predictive analytics, public transportation companies can **predict significant events or days during which they would experience high demand** for services. They can adjust or supplement their facilities accordingly to accommodate visitors better and avoid putting additional cars on the road that cause congestion.

The role and capabilities of transportation management systems (TMS) must continue to evolve and improve as transportation networks and operations become more dynamic and complex. Companies that continue to manage their transportation operations with outdated systems, or worse, with Excel spreadsheets, will find it difficult or impossible to keep pace with their customer requirements, as well as their cost and strategic objectives.

These are the questions that must be asked to determine the best transportation management system available in the age of predictive analytics:

- What factors are driving the need for innovation in transportation management systems?
- What are some of the most important attributes of a next-generation TMS?
- How are emerging technologies like predictive analytics transforming TMS?
- Is access to data and converting it into insights becoming easier?
- Will the role and skills of TMS users need to change too?
- Are next-gen TMS leading to next-gen 3PL relationships?

In today's global, fast-paced world, it's no longer a question of whether an organization should be using technology to manage its supply chain and transportation processes. They should!!! While historically it has been far more common to see medium-sized and large organizations embracing technology to manage their freight activities, today more logistics operations of all sizes are increasing their adoption of tools and technology to solve business problems.

As supply chain/transportation leaders focus on the technologies that can perhaps drive the greatest benefits, one common denominator stands out: data – specifically, how to best manage the growing volume of data. At the core of just about every efficient transportation process is data. The best transportation operations are based on precision and timing, and the same is true of the data they use to drive their decision making. While many decisions rely on instinct or experience, they need to be supported by accurate, timely, and clean data that can be trusted. Without the right technology, collecting and analyzing the vast amounts of data in your supply chain can be difficult, if not impossible.

Using a TMS that pulls in transportation data from across the enterprise is a great starting point to ensure that you have complete and accurate data for making the most-informed decisions for your transportation network. Tiering on a business intelligence tool can help you mine the data, translate it into insights, and deliver information via visual dashboards to drive operational improvements. Business intelligence tools can help you unlock the reservoir of data, analyze it, organize it, and deliver the transportation intelligence you need to the right people.

The best business intelligence tools are those that are arranged to focus on your firm's specific industry, and often are embedded in the system that houses the data to reduce the need to move data to additional tools. It's important to have dashboards that can provide the ability to explore further into the relationships in the information. This facilitates faster answers to the most complicated questions and enables you to make choices that will positively impact your organization's daily workflow.

When the process is working well, all the data captured across the supply chain is continually flowing back to your TMS. Collecting and analyzing your organization's historical data can be crucial for improving and streamlining processes, but applying predictive models to generate forward-looking insights can drive even further improvements.

Predictive analytics may just hold the promise of breaking through what once was thought to be the entirely unpredictable nature of logistics. When it comes to your transportation network, the potential for risk can be hard to anticipate. Using predictive analytics can provide a much higher degree of certainty for impending events based on past data, powerful algorithms, and machine learning. Predictive analytics can help harness demand patterns, capacity levels, product tracking, transportation performance, and product-return activity.

4

TRANSPORTATION IN THE AGE OF ARTIFICIAL INTELLIGENCE

An experimental driver-less truck made by Otto, an Uber-owned company, delivered 50,000 cans of beer after traveling 120 miles at 55 mph from Fort Collins, Colorado, to Colorado Springs. This happened in October 2016. These changes are not just dramatic, they are phenomenal. This beginning will lead us to a different civilization in the coming years and calls for strong global governance. The future of AI in mobility is not just products; it's transportation planning, urban design, real-time traffic management and control, transport policy, environmental issues, AI governance in mobility, and cooperation and collaboration with a lot of entities, in fact all of these things plus more we add in the future.

Autonomous cars and trucks, self-organizing fleets, smart containers, driver-less taxis, and smart cities are just some examples of the reality to come for the transportation industry.

The first iterations of the transition to autonomous cars have already happened: there are cars available in the market, offering advanced active safety systems – technology helping the driver to avoid accidents and risky situations – for example, *auto-breaking, road-sign understanding, lane deviation alerts*, and more.

Due to these artificial intelligence advances, the general feeling is that car interest will shift from **ownership** of a car to **consuming the available car services**. The cost of a *vehicle as a service* will be significantly lower due to, among other factors, the capability of better utilization of the cars by the company operating the service. Combined with the flexibility of *accessing the service* and *planning rides and trips*, the lower cost will make this as-a-service approach very popular and possibly *the primary one*.

Car design, especially the interior will change dramatically, in terms of all *layout and functionality*. Up to now, cars have been developed around **the steering wheel**. In today's cars, the interior of the car is designed and arranged around the driver's position, since it is the driver that must be powered by control and information functions.

In the case of fully autonomous cars, the steering wheel constraint is simply eliminated. This will allow a new approach and *additional degrees of freedom in designing the car's interior*. The **control panel** will have a different shape and positioning, **car seats** can be redesigned and arranged in totally new ways and the car will have its own **digital assistant** while providing context regarding the route, the car, and driving conditions.

Car and truck insurance companies will be significantly impacted since the promise of autonomy is to minimize accidents. The transition to the new era will not be smooth, especially during the co-existence of normal and autonomous transportation methods. This transition will require new processes, new *insurance products, legal adaptation*, and new models to estimate risk. In the case of an accident, the connected mode of transportation will be able to signal the local authorities for help, and also automatically report its state, the conditions under which the accident happened, and all the parameters needed.

This will enable involved parties, including insurance companies, to minimize the effort required to analyze the incident, coordinate the activities, and conclude on responsibilities and claims.

Transportation companies and other companies – including technology startups – are working on the development of autonomous trucks and other vehicles for professional purposes. There are already a number of success stories. Even e-commerce companies like Amazon are automating their delivery systems, as attested to by the development and use of drones in certain areas.

The artificial intelligence revolution will also influence the way cities will grow. For example, the new era of cheaper, faster, and safer transportation with autonomous vehicles might trigger a **de-urbanization trend** – especially if you consider that the time spent in autonomous vehicles can be fully productive with the capabilities of a modern office. One must keep in mind that this type of influence is occurring at the same time the transportation industry is attempting to solve the 'last mile' delivery dilemma.

Changes in the transportation industry will be substantial and notable. On the positive side, we will witness a huge reduction in the number of accidents and fatalities on the roads, thus leading to lower operational costs and increased level of service. On the other hand, technological unemployment will be high while a number of companies will fail to follow and adapt to the new order.

5

THE FINAL-MILE DELIVERY

Even though shipments may be transported over hundreds of miles, or just a few miles, the main focus today is on the final mile – that is, making sure the delivery experience for the end customer is a positive one. What factors are driving this growing attention to final-mile delivery? Why is it important? How can technology, specifically transportation management systems and predictive analytics, help shippers and third-party logistics providers (3PLs) excel in this area?

Discussions about transportation management have traditionally centered on how to get shipments from point A to point B most inexpensively, whether that is across the world, across the country, or within a region. Those discussions have shifted dramatically in the past year or two to focus on final-mile delivery. Why is it such a hot topic today?

There are a number of reasons that the 'last mile' has become so important to the transportation industry for the future of an organization. First, with the fast rise in e-commerce deliveries, whether to homes or businesses, last-mile deliveries are more prevalent and important. Second, companies are realizing the tremendous costs associated with last-mile delivery, which can account for over 30% of the shipping costs. It's also one of the most inefficient parts of delivery. And finally, there is growing awareness that final-mile delivery is the way most people experience a brand and has a profound influence on the perception of the quality of the brand.

Besides the significant cost factor, there are many unique challenges with last-mile deliveries. These can differ in different regions but in urban areas, for one example, one can have road closures, traffic delays, delivery-time restrictions, and parking problems. In rural areas, a lack of density makes deliveries inefficient and time consuming. In both areas, you can have failed deliveries due to no one being available to receive and sign for the delivery. This all adds to the cost. Beyond that, there are challenges from stolen packages, weather issues, returns, and the need for white-glove services for some deliveries.

As with so many challenges in supply chain, we often look to technology to assist. Transportation management systems (TMS) play an important role here. Transportation management systems can better position and aggregate shipments to drop points to shorten last-mile deliveries and times. A TMS can also monitor performance over time for quality and efficiency of service, especially for white-glove service options. It also analyzes costs over the full lifecycle of the order and can determine the full cost to serve and the efficiency of the last-mile segment.

Another challenge is that last-mile deliveries are often performed by a wide range of small couriers and delivery companies that typically have little to no systems support. This is where predictive analytics can help shippers and transportation companies to analyze past trends, including delivery times, quality, and costs, to estimate future needs, to evaluate which couriers to use, and to reroute or change delivery times for better efficiency and service.

Some of the last-mile delivery challenges are the lack of new technology and automation, as well as speed of delivery which leads back to lack of information, on the one hand, and huge data loss, on the other. But, data analytics has become one of the pivotal driving forces in the logistics industry, and its most beneficial elements are when paired with a delivery management software.

A delivery management software should be part of the transportation management system and utilize data analytics to efficiently direct the field workforce and last-mile delivery to their intended destinations, speeding up the delivery process while maintaining the quality of the delivery process. To work smarter and faster, more businesses choose to tap on insights from data so they can then further translate it into real actions and results. This is crucial as companies can now make sure that they fulfill all customer interactions in terms of deliveries and services in the best way possible.

The logistics world is incredibly complex, and technology is driving disruption so fast that companies have to work smarter when trying to reduce operational costs and growing revenue while continuing to improve customer service, revenue and growth at the same time. Today, many companies attempt to optimize their supply chains and operations by using tools such as Excel and assigning their staff to manage the task, but this is an outdated method that doesn't prove to be effective in any way.

However, there are many organizations that utilize supply chain network optimization and analytics to gain insight into their customers and operations that result in those companies becoming leaders in their respective industry. Data analytics is one of the most critical requirements for any business, and many experts will emphasize the importance of leveraging analytics to gain insight and uncover hidden patterns related to processes, customers, and trends.

There are three ways that predictive analytics will assist in the final- or last-mile delivery. They are the following:

1. Improve delivery and performance quality
2. Operational efficiency
3. Improved levels of service

With a predictive analytics module, you'll be able to experience transparency by viewing historical data on orders, drivers, and customers in actionable graphics, making it easier to identify peak hours, seasonality, as well as forecast future delivery needs. This is valuable insight into how you can manage orders in the future as well as gain great feedback that'll help you better coordinate jobs with your staff.

For example, you can also learn how much time and money it takes to serve specific customers in certain parts of cities, or where vehicles run into congestion, resulting in better optimizing routes that will save you money. You can also forecast the likelihood of service issues due to disruptions or unexpected demand spikes.

Data from your route optimization feature, which generates the most optimal route for the vehicle together with the changed rate, becomes incredibly important as it will generate an accurate estimated time and rate in real time. Planning and scheduling deliveries play an important role in the daily life of any supply chain manager, especially because these activities have a direct impact on the overall customer experience.

By using analytics and real-time data collection, staff can plan ahead in terms of demand and delivery efforts, schedule and optimize the transportation routes, improve the number of orders that are on time, and minimize the cost of getting returned items, knowing that problems can be tackled and solved on the go.

As customers dictate the way last-mile delivery happens, companies need to rethink the way they go about daily deliveries. Consumers have higher expectations, and these expectations ultimately influence the overall delivery experience. As more consumers want same-day, and even one-hour, delivery, measuring how quickly a delivery gets to its final destination, from the time it is being dispatched or ordered, the collected data makes for a powerful metric to look at when figuring out how to optimize your supply chain.

Continuing in this vein, of all the steps in an outbound logistical management process, only one step really matters. And that is the final mile, where the customer gets the item in their hands. The customer doesn't care about any other details of the journey. They're not interested in your efficiency metrics or how advanced the technology is. They only care about getting their delivery on time and in perfect condition.

Nobody wants their entire fulfillment process to fall at the last hurdle. That's why final-mile delivery has become an increasingly important focus for logistics companies. If you want to ensure the success of your final-mile delivery, you need a logistics partner that offers visibility and control in the delivery process. These are a few of the metrics you will need:

1. Site profiles
2. Pre-calls
3. Delivery checklists

I will proceed to show how these three will add value to your logistical management strategy.

A good logistics management strategy will adapt to the customer, rather than vice versa. Each end customer has different needs and capabilities, so your final-mile delivery has a better chance of success if you have a clear picture of their requirements.

To do this, you need to build a profile of each site, with as much information as possible about the client, including:

- Hours during which deliveries will be accepted
- Location of delivery entrance
- Vehicle access restrictions
- Security procedures for incoming deliveries
- Special equipment requirements
- Location of persons authorized to sign off on deliveries
- Location of persons who can assist in the event of any queries
- Directions if the site is in a remote or difficult-to-find location
- Any hazards of which the driver may need to be aware
- Any other information that may impact the delivery process

Your final-mile deliverer will need access to this site profile, so that they can get to the right place at the right time without having to stop and make calls for assistance. This makes it more likely that the delivery will be on time and proceed smoothly.

For a first delivery to any site, you will almost certainly want someone from your office to pre-call the site manager and find out as much as possible about the delivery. This will help you to build your initial site profile.

A pre-call will also allow you to discuss things on an individual delivery level. This is especially important if you are dealing with hazardous goods or time-sensitive deliveries.

For final-mile delivery, you should try to speak to the end customer themselves – the person who will ultimately take ownership of the items being transported. They may have to consult over details of the internal logistics procedures of their own organization, but they are still the best person to ensure that the delivery arrives where it needs to go.

Have a checklist ready of questions to ask that will mitigate or prevent any delivery issues:

- Will someone be on site to sign for the delivery?
- Are there any safety precautions that need to be taken with the delivery?
- What safety precautions exist on site?
- For large or complex deliveries, will someone be on site to assist the delivery agent?
- Is there a critical delivery deadline that must be met?
- Is there any other information that may impact the delivery process?

Delivery checklists serve as a client satisfaction survey and as an internal delivery performance metric. By agreeing to the steps of the delivery process in advance, you can ask the client to confirm that all of their expectations were met. Where there is a failure to meet expectations, you can look to improve the process with training, better communication, and building more detailed site profiles.

You might choose to have a single generic checklist, but you should aim to include as much client-specific information as possible. Items on the checklist might include:

- Item loaded to the delivery vehicle as per client instructions
- Delivery arrived within the pre-agreed timeframe
- Items delivered to the correct location, including correct entrance
- All required steps for unloading were followed
- Items received in excellent condition
- Supporting documentation in order and signed by the correct person
- Transportation records provided and contain no anomalies (for cold chain management, etc.)
- Item successfully completed final-mile delivery and was received by the end client

A reason why checklists can become an invaluable internal performance tool is this: clients may not always report back to you if they are dissatisfied with your logistics management. Instead, they may simply vote with their wallet and place their next order with a rival firm. That's why visibility is key to success in final-mile delivery. You need as much practical data as possible to help monitor freight in transit, so that you can see that cargo is arriving on time, in good condition, and according to client requirements. When the process is breaking down, you also need visibility so that you can respond quickly and rectify the situation before it impacts your client relationship.

Your logistics management can't be called successful until the delivery is in the hands of the person who needs it.

6

PREDICTIVE ANALYTICS AND MAINSTREAM BUSINESS TOOLS

We've all been astonished by the promise of what predictive analytics can do – so much so that one of the recent jokes in tech circles is that when startups are asked, 'What's next for your product?' they always blurt out, 'Um, predictive analytics!'

It's easy to see why. The ability for technology to accurately anticipate future needs and serve up appropriate content and solutions seems, well, magical. And as computing power and software continue to evolve, we're seeing companies do increasingly impressive things in the field. Today's solutions are able to derive actionable insights that are being used not only to recommend music and movies but to fight terrorism, forecast the weather, manage employees, and improve health outcomes.

We've already seen huge progress in predictive analytics over the past decade, with several examples capturing headlines. As far back as 2006, Netflix launched a $1 million competition to create a better algorithm for its movie recommendation engine. In 2012, Target was able to correctly guess that a teenage girl was pregnant before her father had a clue – simply by analyzing her shopping habits.

In day-to-day business, however, there have been serious hurdles to making predictive analytics work well in most enterprise environments. The problem isn't what's theoretically possible; it's the limits to what most companies have the ability to implement.

There's also a real lack of critical skills in many enterprises. Predictive analytics skills are in high demand in more than two thirds of organizations. On top of that, there is a dizzying array of choices to help interpret all the data. Software solutions come from a who's who of business intelligence solutions, including IBM, Oracle, SAS, SAP, and countless others.

In short, this is a world where it is easy to get overwhelmed, fall behind, and under-perform. We're now finally starting to see predictive analytics become more accessible and easier to use. Below are five positive trends that will make it easier for enterprises in 2019 and beyond to embrace predictive analytics:

1. **Taxonomy that is more standardized**: often the hardest part about creating good predictive models isn't getting the data or building the model; it's prepping and categorizing the data for analysis. As the field matures, structured data collection will become more standardized and widespread, reducing the time and expense of scrubbing raw data.

2. **More collaboration**: many companies are so ultra-protective of their proprietary predictive tools that insights and methodologies are not shared. That's starting to change as more enterprises insist that their business intelligence partners collaborate more.

3. **More willingness to embrace what's possible with good predictive tools**: I still frequently run into skeptical executives who prefer trusting their gut to trusting 'science'. Those are the folks who will be left behind.

4. **More emphasis on training and data literacy**: many C-suites now include a chief data officer, chief data scientist, or chief analytics officer. This, in turn, has made data literacy a funded priority at most enterprises, and more educational programs are popping up to meet this growing need. I expect the level of data sophistication among enterprise employees will continue to mature in the coming years.

5. **Cheaper tools**: good data storage and analytics tools haven't traditionally been cheap or easy to use. However, there are signs of change. Large companies like Amazon, Google, Facebook, Yahoo, etc., have started to develop scalable storage and computer architecture to help companies manage big data at a fraction of the cost. Predictive analytics tools are sure to follow, increasing in power and decreasing in cost at roughly the rate of Moore's Law.

As part of predictive analytics, business intelligence (BI) is evolving. Business intelligence tools help users answer business questions and measure and monitor business performance at every level of the organization against clearly stated goals and objectives.

Over the years, many firms invested in business intelligence software from multiple suppliers. Often, each department bought its own business intelligence systems, resulting in an explosion of different tools across the business and independent silos. As a result, there is simply too much software out there from different suppliers and no single approach to analyzing data.

A single platform enables organizations to roll out business intelligence tools to a greater cross-section of employees. That is good news for suppliers who sell business intelligence software on a per-seat basis, of course, but it may also be good news for customers who are looking to buy into another key business intelligence trend: performance management.

Regardless of what business intelligence supplier is selected, extending business intelligence to employees at the operational level is becoming vital. However, this is a complex task that few organizations have got right so far. The results of this inequality are clear: top management sets strategic goals for the business, but employees on the lower tiers are unable to work towards them effectively because they are not able to view – and more importantly, act upon – the same information.

For that reason, some companies have established a business intelligence competency center – a cross-functional team of employees from both IT and other parts of the business. This center is responsible for supporting and promoting the use of business intelligence tools by employees.

A prime example of a company attempting to set up such a center and encountering some difficulties was Electrolux, the Swedish home appliance firm. The company's project, based on Cognos business intelligence technology, has come up against a number of challenges since it was launched two years ago. The two primary impediments were:

1. Getting funding to set up the center. A business intelligence competency center is an enterprise-wide effort and requires enterprise-wide support and champion
2. 'Selling' the concept of such a center to a large organization where previously business intelligence was structured by divisions or subsidiaries

Employees in different countries and different business units were used to developing and using their own business intelligence systems and were inclined to protect those tools. They were also very protective of what they perceived as their 'ownership' of information. However, Electrolux has managed to outline a roadmap for existing business intelligence tools and embarked on a data integration project that will enable Electrolux employees to view profit information down to product level.

Despite these headaches, Electrolux is confident that the business intelligence competency center will pay off in the long run, enabling Electrolux employees in sales, marketing, finance, and manufacturing across multiple territories to access a single view of corporate performance.

The business information center is the only way to achieve a single version of the truth and the only way we will ever be able to compare accurately the business performance of individual business units.

7

USING PREDICTIVE ANALYTICS TO DRIVE SALES AND CUSTOMER SERVICE

Predictive analytics is changing the customer-seller relationship, improving sales while increasing shopper satisfaction at the same time.

This is all possible because of business's new superpower – data. Business analytics gives you the ability to see and predict everything – every interaction with customers, every moving part in your supply chain, and every financial transaction anywhere in the world. In the retail industry, predictive analytics provides sellers a new advantage, one that more than compensates for the Internet's ever-expanding array of choices.

Predictive analytics help you know what might happen, prepare a response ahead of time, get ahead of the risks, and influence the outcomes. It's like looking ahead with a telescope, not glancing through the rear-view mirror.

If you still have doubts that predictive analytics isn't the most powerful marketing tool since the entry of online shopping, then consider these seven ways your firm can use the technology to take customer service and sales to the next level.

1. Hyper-personalized marketing:

   Hyper-personalized marketing is all about serving customers with the right message at the right time on the right channel.

   Getting it right requires a merger of arts and science. The science part is giving shoppers the right mix of categories, selections, price points, shipping times, and other key services. The arts come into play when we determine how we curate these elements, how we entwine them together to create the most engaging customer experience.

   Imagine if the retailer knows exactly what a shopper wants even before arriving on the company's website or app. That's a capability predictive analytics can provide. Through data-driven technology, we can create a personalized collection, incorporating thousands of products, every single day.

   For the first time in history, social media and other online avenues allow marketers to interact with people anytime, anywhere. This provides an unmatched opportunity to discover the emerging patterns that help companies position their resources and direct their energies more effectively. By collecting all these little points of data around the customer experience and integrating them together, we can get a better picture of the complete customer journey.

2. Virtual concierges:

   Consumers have come to expect instant gratification in all aspects of their lives and now expect similar experiences with the brands they interact with. Predictive analytics is a critical tool in delivering a comprehensive view of the consumer to provide these types of experiences.

3. Customer needs forecasting:

   Organizations can now use predictive analytics to precisely forecast customers' needs, in some cases even before the individual has made up his or her mind. Predictive analytics can provide early detection of precursors to change in customer behavior. This allows brands to be more proactive, enabling them to tailor their messages in anticipation, effectively serving the customer before they even know they have a new need. It's an approach that allows organizations to provide superior customer service.

Predictive analytics helps companies ensure they have the right amount of support in place to address customers' needs in a timely fashion and then exceed their expectations. Looking to get inside its customers' heads, some companies have implemented a customer experience machine learning system. The technology digests hundreds of unique data elements throughout customer project lifecycles.

4. Customer churn reduction:

Retailers have long searched for ways of reducing customer churn, that is, the percentage of once loyal customers who have stopped acquiring a company's products or services during a specific time frame. Also known as customer attrition, customer churn is a critical metric, given that it's far less expensive to retain existing customers than it is to acquire new ones.

Predictive analytics can be used to identify customers presenting a high churn risk and help businesses take proactive attention to enhance customer experience and serve their needs better. Disaffected customers can often be lured back into the fold with incentives, such as time payment plans or lower price alternatives.

Analytics-delivered clues, such as a denied loan request, can alert a bank or other financial institution to customers presenting a high churn risk. Upon learning this information, the financial institution could then act pre-emptively to prevent customer churn by offering additional options, like a credit card with a generous limit.

5. Resources management:

Predictive analytics can also help companies in allocating their resources more wisely and productively. It can help retailers combine insight from their store footprints, logistics, and customer behavior to accurately plan staffing levels, weeks in advance. This will enable customers to have a smooth, better, and faster experience with that retailer.

Using predictive models, sellers can create accurate inventory forecasts and manage resources to match customer behaviors and needs. The benefits are twofold, companies can be more efficient, streamlining costs and reducing wasted resources, and customers receive the timely and personalized experiences that they have come to expect.

6. Internal team support:

Predictive analytics gives internal support teams the insights needed to resolve customer problems quickly and accurately. It's a key tool in the arsenal to better understand and improve the customer experience.

By drawing on predictive analytics fed by phone calls, emails, social media sentiment, customer escalations, and other key channels, any company representatives can determine the best way to address specific types of customer demands. Taking all of these inputs into account helps us to be more prepared to address customer needs and make better business decisions. Predictive analytics helps to ensure we have the right amount of support in place to address customers' needs in a timely fashion and exceed their expectations.

7. Smooth shipping:

Predictive analytics enables organizations to enhance the customer experience all the way up to delivery day. With more customers demanding next-day and same-day deliveries, predictive analytics helps retailers and their shipping partners ensure reliable, on-time arrivals.

By forecasting potential maintenance issues and pinpointing optimal transport routes, predictive analytics now plays a major role in ensuring that delivery schedules are met on time. Analytics allow for each driver to have better expectations about their journey, and transportation departments can communicate earlier what adjustments need to be made on transport routes to manage volume, thereby impacting experience.

Since we are dealing with humans in the transportation and delivery of the product to the customer and or consumer – who is also human – we are presented with a question or dilemma. How and what are the human factors affecting the digitalization of the supply chain?

Part 9

THE HUMAN FACTORS IN SUPPLY CHAIN DIGITALIZATION

Global supply chains are evolving into vigorous networks in which companies connect in unique combinations based on the context and requirements of individual projects. This dynamic environment requires effective communication, team management, and constant lifecycle innovation. Human factor insights in these areas are critical for the effective development of global process networks. Successful companies are those that consider their human capital as their most important asset. Facts and figures are important considerations of successful management, yet the cognitive aspects are those that actually make or break an organization. Assuming that the employees of an organization in supply chains are individuals with own sensitivities, own goals, and own personalities the organization should be able to employ both individual and group psychology in order to commit employees to the achievement of organizational goals.

Understanding the human factors in the 21st-century supply chain is the inevitable outgrowth of what was formerly called 'employee engagement'. The human factor is a strategic approach for the management of an organization's most precious assets – the employees working there who individually and collectively contribute to the achievement of the objectives of the business. This includes developing their capacities and utilizing and maintaining and compensating their services in tune with the job and organizational needs and requirements.

1

ARE HUMAN JOBS AT RISK WITH SUPPLY CHAIN AUTOMATION?

At one time, our culture was obsessed with cyborgs named Arnold and systems named Skynet. Artificial intelligence was still largely theory and amusement for most people. Fast forward to today, when AI and robotics are normal – no one bats an eye when asking Alexa to buy toner on Amazon.

Hollywood may have moved on from the Terminator to a host of different villains, but do AI and robotics cause those in supply chain management to fear that ultimately their jobs will be 'terminated'? (No pun intended.) To be sure, there is a level of optimism on the tech's returns, but there are those who do not always share it. Many humans are asking, will automation truly phase out the need for our services?

From a supply chain management standpoint, automation removes errors their carbon-based counterparts are quick to create, and there isn't constant training or re-training to improve work efficiency. 'Teach' a robot once, via coding, and it continues to perform until the technology is surpassed or improved upon or there is physically an issue with it.

Productivity, efficiency, the lack of downtime needed for human concerns like eating and sleep – automation sounds like a dream for engineers focused on speed and efficiency.

But is supply chain automation really the cure-all it purports to be?

Humans are still necessary for every aspect of supply chain management, no matter how advanced the automation becomes. Regardless of how much programming is done, there will be a situation in which human judgment is needed. For example, automation in a sorter may be able to recognize a label on a box, but if the associates there know the customer wants their product, even boxes, in pristine condition, they have the capability to pull it off and correct the order. Sure, technically it was right – but when dealing with customers, you can't be just 'technically right'. Quality is a collection of standards, to be certain, but ultimately it is defined by the customer – and each customer is different.

Just as no man is an island, any AI needs a human to coordinate everything from programming cycle time to maintenance schedules. In this capacity, automation actually can create more jobs in maintenance and engineering, not sacrifice them. In fact, college students looking to enter the supply chain sphere have a host of new vocational opportunities in their hands – the pneumatic arms of these new, hardworking machines as the technology continues to gain momentum. A four-year degree may no longer be in demand, so how about a Vo-tech degree in maintenance or mechanics? This could be the ticket to the future. As AI technology improves, we will need more people to service the machines for the supply chain to keep humming along.

So the question still remains: What jobs will remain and which jobs will disappear?

When you walk into the warehouse of the future, the workforce will look different. It will not always be pleasant, but as technology advances, there are jobs that will fall by the wayside. In the future, AI in the form of sorters will be able to pick a product, thus eliminating the former necessary position of the warehouse picker. These positions are heavily manual and don't necessarily require an advanced skill set. However, there will still need to be the need for entry labor warehouse positions, but in different roles that complement their skill level. Certification, degrees, and specializations are the best protectors against 'job outsourcing'. Human-centric career paths, such as human resources, leadership roles, maintenance, and quality can't be so easily replicated by wires and solenoids. Efficiency alone isn't enough these days, and managers must identify and create new positions to usher in both automation and the maintenance required to keep it running.

Positions that already rely on computers, such as oversight, sales, and lead generation, will stay in the coming tide of automation. The human element can make a big difference – particularly in B2B and B2C outreach and delivery. Other jobs that will only increase include systems engineering and quality engineering to make sure the AI technology is functioning as it should.

While we can automate site features like shipment updates – removing the burden from a live customer service agent – don't expect to opt out of direct customer assistance just yet. Instead, the scope of their job could widen, especially in the face of remote management and 'back-end' capabilities from a home laptop or desktop. This wider variety of data points can also represent a liability for cyber-attacks, so make sure your network is secure before uploading live invoicing data or accessing sensitive data.

Imagine the face of a supply chain when readily available automated truck driving is an option for delivery. A company wouldn't have to wait for the next round of cargo pickups, and the truck could drive through the night without needing to stop for sleep or food. This doesn't mean the end of human truck drivers, however; a human attendant will likely have to tag along for liability reasons, ready to take the wheel if an automated engine were to falter in its duties or become compromised through hacking efforts.

Since every company is concerned about quality or at least they should be, they might ask how we can connect the dots to quality. Quality should be viewed holistically – knowing that each part of a company affects the other and putting in processes and improvements that streamline work across those parts. AI that prevents cyber-attacks from crippling hardware in an automated truck is a part of the quality system, ensuring customers are receiving product quickly and safely. Removing human error from a picking and sorting process through AI is an improvement to quality. Quality is more than just documents and records, it's a transformative mindset that is always seeking to add value to customers, and if quality is not as important as it should be in your company's culture, you will be late to the game when it comes to AI technology.

To borrow a phrase from Aldous Huxley – this brave new world may come to fruition in as little as a decade. The timeline largely depends on the level of investment for expenditures on robots and programming at top companies. The best results also come from a network of companies all using the same or similar automation – trading best practices, highlighting concerns, and discovering the best placement for automated components on the warehouse floor.

The pressure from clients to move towards automation could affect supply chain partner behavior, too. If we keep transparency at the forefront, automation could be within reach sooner rather than later. If, however, companies remain hesitant and cautious, preferring instead to lean on familiar practices over new ones, your road to automation may take the scenic route.

2

HUMAN FACTOR ENGINEERING IN SUPPLY CHAIN AUTOMATION

Before we enter into a discussion about how human factor engineering (HFE) assists in supply chain automation, we must define the term and explain how it works.

Human factors engineering is the discipline that takes into account human strengths and limitations in the design of interactive systems that involve people, tools, and technology, and work environments to ensure safety, effectiveness, and ease of use. A human factors engineer examines a particular activity in terms of its component tasks, and then assesses the physical demands, skill demands, mental workload, team dynamics, aspects of the work environment, and device design required to complete the task optimally. In essence, human factors engineering focuses on how systems work in actual practice, with real – and fallible – human beings at the controls, and attempts to design systems that optimize safety and minimize the risk of error in complex environments.

Human factors engineering has long been used to improve safety in many industries. It has been employed to analyze errors in aviation, automobiles, and the Three Mile Island nuclear power plant accident. In other industries it has lagged behind and only now struggling to catch up.

The very nature of human factors engineering rules out 'one size fits all' solutions, but several tools and techniques are commonly used as human factors approaches to addressing safety issues. They are the following:

- Usability testing: human factors engineers test new systems and equipment under real-world conditions as much as possible, in order to identify potential problems and unintended consequences of new technology. One prominent example of the clinical applicability of *usability testing* involves electronic medical records. A recent example discussed a serious medication overdose that occurred in part due to confusing displays in an institution's medical records – a vivid example of how failing to use human factors engineering principles in user-interface design can potentially harm patients.

- Forcing functions: an aspect of a design that prevents an unintended or undesirable action from being performed or allows its performance only if another specific action is performed first. For example, automobiles are now designed so that the driver cannot shift into reverse without first putting his or her foot on the brake pedal. Forcing functions need not involve device design. One of the first forcing functions identified in health care was the removal of concentrate potassium from general hospital wards. This action helps prevent the inadvertent addition of concentrated potassium to intravenous solutions prepared by nurses on the wards, an error that has produced small but consistent numbers of deaths for many years.

- Standardization: an axiom of human factors engineering is that equipment and processes should be standardized whenever possible, in order to increase reliability, improve information flow, and minimize cross-training needs. Standardized processes are increasingly being implemented as safety measures. The widening use of checklists as a means of ensuring that safety steps are performed in the correct order has its roots in human factors engineering principles.

- Resiliency efforts: given that unexpected events are likely to occur, attention needs to be given to their detection and mitigation before they worsen. Rather than focus on error and design efforts to preclude it, resiliency approaches tap into the dynamic aspects of risk management, exploring how organizations anticipate and adapt to changing conditions and recover from system anomalies. Building on insights from high-reliability organizations, complex adaptive systems, and resourceful providers at the point of care, resilience is viewed as a critical system property, reflecting the organization's capacity to bounce back in the face of continuing pressures and challenges when the margins of safety have become thin.

Despite the above examples, it is generally agreed that human factors principles are underutilized in examination of safety problems and in designing potential solutions.

Why should you care about completing human factors engineering (HFE) in relation to your supply chain? Simple: humans are involved. At every stage of your medical device's lifecycle, there are people participating in assembly, handling, packing, and so on.

Particularly during manufacturing, your team wants to focus on HFE exercises to help control risks that could arise in later lifecycle stages. But what manufacturing steps should be evaluated with human factors in mind? There are three manufacturing steps which should be evaluated with human factors in mind. The three are as follows:

- Following process controls: when reaching the end of your product development, your team should be finalizing methods and process controls for building your device. These must include things such as what equipment is used, who is qualified to build which parts, the order in which devices are assembled, and so on. These controls are especially important when manufacturing and supply are contracted out; a third party understands the vision of your product less than you do, so you need to be clear when giving them the data necessary to build the product. If these processes are unclear, incomprehensive, or lack thorough risk controls, there is plenty of room for error to occur. While much of the process for building hardware is now automated, humans administer or even physically finalize builds. Even in a device that's primarily software based, any number of vague or unclear directions could result in the wrong software being installed.
- Understanding testing protocols: testing is perhaps one of the most important parts of the manufacturing process. Prior to delivery to a

user, devices need to be tested to ensure proper operation and quality. Your team wants to be certain the right testing thresholds and methods are in place so that users receive properly assembled, fully functional devices. This can help identify issues such as ones that might arise from faulty process controls. However, just like process controls, testing protocols need to be clear. When they aren't, the likelihood of human error occurring during manufacturing increases. A perfect example of the above is this: your team may write up an executable test to confirm the power button on the device is fully functional. They give work instructions for testers to follow and validation criteria that the device must meet before it can be supplied to users. If there is room for interpretation in the test process or unclear validation criteria, testers are more likely to incorrectly execute and document their results. Approaching these issues from an HFE perspective can reduce their likelihood of occurrence and ensure device safety throughout the product lifecycle.

- Packaging/labeling instructions: here are untold numbers of errors that could impact device safety when it comes to packaging and labeling. Improper packaging and subsequent shipping could damage the device; incorrectly labeled functions on a device or dosing that accompanies a combination product can severely jeopardize user safety; even vague instructions about shipping packaged devices could expose users to risk. When human errors in these processes are not evaluated, the safety of a user can be put at risk.

When we look at error in the overall supply chain, the processes involving humans during manufacturing and delivery need to be scrutinized. Automation is taking over production faster than before, but humans are still involved with the process at some level. Using HFE exercises early on to assess where human errors in manufacturing can occur then results in optimized production time and decreased risk for all involved.

3

BUT, WILL WE STILL NEED PEOPLE?

Per a *Washington Post* article dated November 30, 2017, this austere news-paper is predicting this:

Robots Replace Nearly a Third of U.S. Workers by the Year 2030

That is one take on the growth of automation, but there are other sides to the story.

However, from a Gartner study called '2019 Magic Quadrant' and the Bureau of Labor Occupational Statistics quite another story is being painted.

The modern economy was built on automation, so it's natural to assume that the future will be defined by automation as well. It seems like every week there's a new study about the job-destroying potential of robotics and artificial intelligence. But our collective obsession with job-stealing robots can cause us to overestimate the impact of automation and obscure an important point about the economy. In many service industries, human labor is a mark of luxury.

So at the same time robots destroy manufacturing jobs, the demand for labor-intensive services is soaring.

We can see the signs of this all around us. There's the rise of Etsy, an online marketplace whose main selling point is that the products are not mass-produced. There's the craze for restaurants with organic, locally sourced ingredients that often come from smaller, less mechanized farms. There's the unexpected rise in the number of small wineries and breweries where a personal touch – and often a tour of the facilities – is a big part of the selling point (see Figure 9.3.1).

Companies are using their lack of automation as a selling point. They're doing this because customers like the feeling of a personal connection to the farmers, brewers, and artisans who make the products they're buying.

As automation makes everyday products cheaper and more plentiful, people will increasingly shift their spending to goods and services where a connection to a human provider is seen as a key benefit.

Perhaps, nowhere is this more visible than with Starbucks.

Starbucks management understood something important about their business: people don't go to Starbucks simply to get a cup of coffee – after

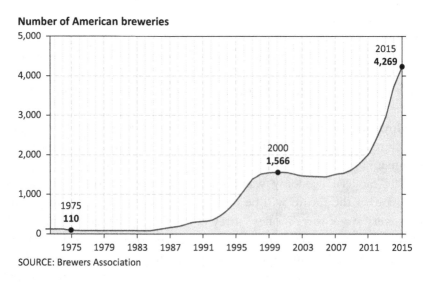

Figure 9.3.1 Increase in the number of American breweries between 1975 and 2015

all, there are lots of cheaper and faster ways to get coffee. People go to Starbucks because they enjoy the experience. And that experience has an important performance-based dimension – customers want to feel like their barista devoted personal attention to preparing their cup.

Starbucks is hardly the most upscale coffee shop around. Serious coffee snobs refuse to drink the stuff, preferring independent coffee shops with exotic fair-trade beans. The process of making coffee at these stores is often even more elaborate and labor intensive than at Starbucks. These shops are often smaller and don't have the Starbucks brand pulling in customers; baristas tend to serve fewer customers – often leading to higher prices.

The fastest-growing occupations are mostly service-oriented
Projected by the Labor Department

	Growth rate, 2014–'24	2015 median pay per year
Wind turbine service technicians	108%	$51,050
Occupational therapy assistants	43%	$57,870
Physical therapist assistants	41%	$55,170
Physical therapist aides	39%	$25,120
Home health aides	38%	$21,920
Commercial divers	37%	$50,470
Nurse practitioners	35%	$98,190
Physical therapists	34%	$84,020
Statisticians	34%	$80,110
Ambulance drivers and attendants	33%	$23,740
Occupational therapy aides	31%	$27,800
Physician assistants	30%	$98,180
Operations research analysts	30%	$78,630
Personal financial advisers	30%	$89,160
Cartographers	29%	$61,880
Genetic counselors	29%	$72,090
Interpreters and translators	29%	$44,190
Audiologists	29%	$74,890
Hearing aid specialists	27%	$49,600
Optometrists	27%	$103,900

0   25   50   75   100

SOURCE: Bureau of Labor Statistics

Figure 9.3.2 US Labor Department's projections for the fastest-growing occupations between 2014 and 2024

A lot of coffee lovers don't care. They believe that elaborately prepared artisanal coffee is better than the mass-market stuff, and they're willing to pay a premium for it. This helps explain why there continues to be a big market for people to make coffee, even while coffee machines get even more sophisticated.

Coffee is far from the most important industry in the US. But similar trends can be seen in large areas of the American economy. One way to see this is by looking at the US Labor Department's occupation projections of the fastest-growing occupations between 2014 and 2024. A bunch of slots are taken up by therapists and caretakers: physical therapists and their aides and assistants, occupational therapy aides and assistants, home health aides, etc. (see Figure 9.3.2).

Over time, technological progress is steadily wringing inefficiencies out of manufacturing processes. But in service-related industries, the 'inefficiencies' involved in talking to other people are often a key benefit. So as America continues to get richer, we should expect these services to account for a larger and larger share of economic activity.

4

WHAT IMPACT WILL AUTOMATION HAVE UPON WAREHOUSE WORKERS?

The modern-day warehouse is serving as a testing ground for the introduction of innovative supply chain technologies. But the implications for human workers remain uncertain. Automation is transforming virtually every aspect of warehouse and distribution center operations. The age of e-commerce demands unprecedented levels of efficiency and speed of order fulfillment.

Software is playing a major role in driving new advances in the warehouse. Perhaps ten years ago, the technology you selected would be the driving force for design, but now we tend to start with software and studying processes.

The rising cost of labor is another factor in the push for greater automation. Over the past year, declining unemployment rates and a rise in the minimum wage have only aggravated the situation for employers. In addition, the growth of the 'gig economy' has created a less reliable labor pool, with employers struggling to staff up during periods of peak demand.

Wage levels aside, the business case for automation is strong, noting that new systems improve accuracy, safety, and inventory management, while reducing facility downtime.

Of all recent technological advances, robotics is having the most direct impact on the human workforce.

The rapid adoption of robots throughout the warehouse has led to sharp reductions in staffing. But the choice doesn't necessarily come down to one of robots or humans. The emergence of 'cobots' has created an environment where humans and machines work side by side, each attending to its natural strengths.

Where an automated system chooses to store inventory often differs sharply from the decisions made by legacy technology. Systems driven by artificial intelligence can account for multiple factors, to the point where the logic of placement might not be evident to the human eye. The result is a facility that's more responsive to the needs of the moment.

The job of the remaining humans in the warehouse, at least for now, is to follow the machine's directions on where to locate and pick product. Robots then convey the goods to the packing station or dock for loading onto trucks – once again, by humans.

This is made possible by new designs that allow for people and robots to operate safely in proximity to one another. Previously in warehouses and factories, robots had to be segregated in cages or sequestered areas of the facility. New models are equipped with vision systems and other devices that prevent them from harming humans.

Full automation of the warehouse, isn't necessarily the goal. If you can automate 80% of the volume, the remaining 20% might consist of small steps or value-added functions that are not easily automated. They are especially common in e-commerce fulfillment environments, where personal touches to packaging and other elements of the order are often called for.

It could be two to three decades before fully automated warehouses are the norm. Nevertheless, there remains the question of what to do with those workers who have been displaced by automation. Many will need to be re-trained or shifted to other trades entirely. The types of skills needed for software engineers and systems designers aren't often found in the worker on the warehouse floor.

Because the average worker today is savvier about information technology, re-training might become more of an option in future. A forklift mechanic, for example, could undergo training in the controls of automated guided vehicles (AGVs).

Yet the ultimate fate of the human worker remains in doubt. Automation is sure to take over an increasing number of tasks within distribution centers. 'Intelligent' systems will only get smarter. Where people fit into that picture is a question that could remain unanswered for years to come.

5

THE ROLE OF HUMAN FACTORS ON THE FUTURE OF MANUFACTURING

For new systems to be successful, we need to ensure that people are not only able but keen to work with them. Technology is at the forefront of all new manufacturing design processes, and in a relatively short space of time, has seen exponential growth, impacting immensely on almost everything that we do as part of our everyday lives, including how we work.

In recent years, the adoption of digitalization and automation has grown across many industrial sectors but humans often bear the brunt of responsibility when errors arise. A key aspect of getting the design of the latest technologies right, and to determine how successful they will be, is how well we understand how they will impact and can be assimilated with human workforces.

As levels of automation, informatics, robotics, sensors, and mobile devices increase, it is particularly important to remember that human skills will still remain essential for many tasks, making the marriage between humans and machines critical to success. Human factors will therefore play an essential role in the future of technological advances, where people and technology are being integrated more closely and more intensively than ever before. Thus, it becomes essential that we completely understand how to design and functionalize both human and technological aspects of the business.

Human factors provide a scientific approach to human-centered design, using physiological and psychological principles to optimize people's strengths and limitations. It has a long-standing history of making important contributions to manufacturing technologies and processes, although often as a limited part of engineering design, and too late in the design process to have an impact. The current challenge for industry is to include human factors with engineering and technology developments in order to optimize how workforces and infrastructure are prepared for the transformational changes brought about by digitalization.

The application of human factors in design activities is vital to ensure that we are creating robots that can effectively and safely work and interact with people. For example, humans come in all shapes and sizes and, unlike machines, bring high levels of unpredictability in their responses and behavior. Human variability has been a traditional problem for the technology industry but the progressive trend for more flexible and adaptable workforces means that differences between the workforce and their capabilities is being seen as more valuable in systems which require more frequent product and skills changes. Humans are able to respond to unusual or unexpected situations, and contribute towards the resilience of a system. So, as workforces become more mobile, diverse, and dependent on technology, human factors are needed to ensure the inclusive design of robots and smart systems to improve their capability for interpreting and responding to human necessities.

For implementation purposes, an important role for human factors is to assist in the design of the workforce introduction, operator training, and other strategies that will enhance people's willingness to engage with robotics and automation. Worker acceptance is always critical to the success of new technology adoption, so if we are now facing the prospect of installing automation, which requires greater levels of communication and collaboration with the human worker, then it is clearly going to be even more imperative that we are better equipped to ensure that people understand how technologies are changing the workplace, and work towards acceptance of these technologies.

Future workplaces are going to look very different, and it is important that we consider the implications for design and implementation. Although it is expected that future workforces will be more mobile, it is also important to consider how to prepare existing workers who will be called upon to adapt their tasks, techniques, processes, and cultures. The application of human factors is the most appropriate approach for redeveloping and enhancing manual and cognitive skill sets, to prepare workers for changing work environments and new task demands in future production systems. For new systems to be successful, we need to ensure that people are not only able but keen to work with them, and that the technologies genuinely enhance jobs and have a positive impact on workplace productivity and satisfaction.

GLOSSARY

Artificial intelligence   In computer science, artificial intelligence (AI), sometimes called machine intelligence, is intelligence demonstrated by machines, in contrast to the natural intelligence displayed by humans. Leading AI textbooks define the field as the study of 'intelligent agents': any device that perceives its environment and takes actions that maximize its chance of successfully achieving its goals. The term 'artificial intelligence' is often used to describe machines (or computers) that mimic 'cognitive' functions that humans associate with the human mind, such as learning and problem solving.

ABC analysis   In materials management, the *ABC analysis* is an inventory categorization technique. The ABC analysis divides an inventory into three categories – 'A items' with very tight control and accurate records, 'B items' with less tightly controlled and good records, and 'C items' with the simplest controls possible and minimal records.

   The ABC analysis provides a mechanism for identifying items that will have a significant impact on overall inventory cost, while also providing a mechanism for identifying different categories of stock that will require different management and controls.

Advanced shipping notice (ASN)   It is a notification of pending deliveries, similar to a packing list. It is usually sent in an electronic format. The ASN can be used to list the contents of a shipment of goods as well as additional information relating to the shipment, such as order information, product description, physical characteristics, type of packaging, markings, carrier information, and configuration of goods within the transportation equipment. The ASN enables the sender to describe the contents and configuration of a shipment in various levels of detail and provides an ordered flexibility to convey information

Alignment   The process in which a business organization uses information technology to achieve business objectives – typically improved financial performance or marketplace competitiveness. Some definitions focus more on outcomes: the harmony between IT and business decision makers within the organizations.

Blockchain   A blockchain is a growing list of records called *blocks* that are linked using cryptography. Each block contains a cryptographic hash of the previous block, a timestamp, and transaction data.

By design, a blockchain is resistant to modification of the data. It is an open, distributed ledger that can record transactions between two parties efficiently and in a verifiable and permanent way. For use as a ledger, a blockchain is typically managed by a peer-to-peer network collectively adhering to a protocol for inter-node communication and validating new blocks. Once recorded, the data in any given block cannot be altered retroactively without alteration of all subsequent blocks, which requires consensus of the network majority.

Buffer inventory   Buffer inventory, also known as safety stock, is a term used by logisticians to describe a level of extra stock that is maintained to mitigate risk of stock outs or a shortfall in raw material or packaging caused by uncertainties in supply and demand. Adequate safety stock levels permit business operations to proceed according to their plans. Safety stock is held when uncertainty exists in demand, supply, or manufacturing yield, and serves as an insurance against stock outs.

Business intelligence   It comprises the strategies and technologies used by enterprises for the data analysis of business information. BI, for short, technologies provide historical, current, and predictive views of business operations. Common functions of business intelligence technologies include reporting, online analytical processing, data mining, business performance management, benchmarking, or metrics. BI technologies can handle large amounts of structured and sometimes unstructured data to help identify, develop, and otherwise create new strategic business opportunities.

Cloud computing   It is the on-demand availability of computer system resources, especially data storage and computing power, without direct active management by the user. The term is generally used to describe data centers available to many users over the Internet. Large clouds, predominant today, often have functions distributed over multiple locations from central servers. Clouds may be limited to a single organization, or be available to many organizations.

Cobots   Cobots, or collaborative robots, are robots intended to interact with humans in a shared space or to work safely in close proximity. Cobots stand in contrast to traditional industrial robots which are designed to work autonomously with safety assured by isolation from human contact. Cobot safety may rely on lightweight construction materials, rounded edges, and limits on speed or force. Safety may also require sensors and software to assure good collaborative behavior.

Continuous process improvement   It refers to an ongoing effort to improve products, services, or processes. This effort can seek incremental improvement over time or breakthrough improvement all at once. Delivery of customer valued processes are constantly evaluated and improved in the light of their efficiency, effectiveness, and flexibility.

Customer value   Customer value is the value received by the end customer of a product or service. End customer can include a single individual or an organization with various individuals playing different roles in the buying/consumption processes. Customer value is conceived variously as utility, quality, benefits, and customer satisfaction

Cycle time   It is a measure of the total elapsed time to complete an operation or set of operations. Order cycle time can now be minutes.

Data science   A concept used to unify statistics, data analysis, machine learning, and their related methods in order to understand and analyze actual phenomena with data. It employs techniques and theories drawn from many fields within the context of mathematics, statistics, computer science, and information science.

Demand sensing   It is a forecasting method that leverages new mathematical techniques and near real-time information to create an accurate forecast of demand, based on the current realities of the supply chain. Traditionally, forecasting accuracy was based on time series techniques which create a forecast based on prior sales history and draws on several years of data to provide insights into predictable seasonal patterns. However, past sales are frequently a poor predictor of future sales. Demand sensing is fundamentally different in that it uses a much broader range of demand signals and different mathematics to create a more accurate forecast that responds to real-world events such as market shifts, weather changes, natural disasters, consumer buying behavior, etc.

Enterprise resource planning   ERP is usually referred to as a category of business management software, typically a suite of integrated applications, that an organization can use to collect, store, manage, and interpret data from many business activities.

The Five Whys   They are questions whose answers are considered basic in information gathering or problem solving. They are often mentioned in journalism, business research, and police investigations. According to the principle of the Five Ws, a report can only be considered complete if it answers these questions: Who, What, When, Where, and Why.

Flowcharts   It is a type of diagram that represents a workflow or process. A flowchart can also be defined as a diagrammatic representation of an algorithm, a step-by-step approach to solving a task.

The flowchart shows the steps as boxes of various kinds, and their order by connecting the boxes with arrows. This diagrammatic representation illustrates a solution model to a given problem. Flowcharts are used in analyzing, designing, documenting, or managing a process or program in various fields.

Gross domestic product   It is a monetary measure of the market value of all the final goods and services produced in a specific time period. GDP does not reflect differences in the cost of living and the inflation rates of the countries; therefore, using a basis of GDP per capita at purchasing power is more useful when comparing living standards between nations.

Human factor engineering   This is the application of psychological and physiological principles to the engineering and design of products, processes, and systems. The goal of human factors is to reduce human error, increase productivity, and enhance safety and comfort with a specific focus on the interaction between the human and the thing of interest.

Industry 4.0 It is the subset of the fourth industrial revolution that concerns industry. The fourth industrial revolution encompasses areas which are not normally classified as an industry, such as smart cities.

Although the terms 'Industry 4.0' and 'fourth industrial revolution' are often used interchangeably, 'Industry 4.0' factories have machines which are augmented with wireless connectivity and sensors, connected to a system that can visualize the entire production line and make decisions on its own.

Jidoka It is a feature of machine design. It may be described as automation with a human touch. This type of automation implements some supervisory functions rather than production functions. At Toyota, this usually means that if an abnormal situation arises, the machine stops and the worker will stop the production line. It is a quality control process that applies the following four principles:
1. Detect the abnormality.
2. Stop.
3. Fix or correct the immediate condition.
4. Investigate the root cause and install a countermeasure.

Just-in-time It is a methodology aimed primarily at reducing times within the production system as well as response times from suppliers and to customers. Its origin and development was in Japan, largely in the 1960s and 1970s and particularly at Toyota.

Kaizen It is a concept referring to business activities that continuously improve all functions and involve all employees from the CEO to the assembly line workers. It is the Sino-Japanese word for improvement. Kaizen also applies to processes, such as purchasing and logistics, that cross organizational boundaries into the supply chain.

Key performance indicators KPIs evaluate the success of an organization or of a particular activity (such as projects, programs, products, and other initiatives) in which it engages.

Lean It is a business methodology that aims to provide a new way to think about how to organize human activities to deliver more

benefits to society and value to individuals while eliminating waste. The term 'lean thinking' was coined by James P. Womack to capture the essence of their in-depth study of Toyota's fabled Toyota Production System. Lean thinking is a way of thinking about an activity and seeing the waste inadvertently generated by the way the process is organized. It uses the concepts of:
1. Value
2. Value streams
3. Flow

Level production schedule Also known as production smoothing, it is a technique for reducing the unevenness which in turn reduces waste. It was vital to the development of production efficiency in the Toyota Production System and lean manufacturing. The goal is to produce intermediate goods at a constant rate so that further processing may also be carried out at a constant and predictable rate.

Machine learning It is the scientific study of algorithms and statistical models that computer systems use to perform a specific task without using explicit instructions, relying on patterns. It is seen as a subset of artificial intelligence. Machine learning algorithms build a mathematical model based on sample data, known as training data, in order to make predictions or decisions without being explicitly programmed to perform the task.

Manufacturing execution systems (MES) They are computerized systems used in manufacturing to track and document the transformation of raw materials to finished goods. MES provides information that helps manufacturing decision makers understand how current conditions on the plant floor can be optimized to improve production output. MES works in real time to enable the control of multiple elements of the production process (e.g. inputs, personnel, machines, and support services).

Material resource planning It is defined as a method for the effective planning of all resources of a manufacturing company. Ideally, it addresses operational planning in units, financial planning, and has a simulation capability to answer 'what-if' questions.

Omnichannel It is a cross-channel content strategy that organizations use to improve their user experience and drive better relationships with their audience across points of contact. Rather than working in parallel, communication channels and their supporting resources are designed and orchestrated to cooperate. Omnichannel implies integration and orchestration of channels such that the experience of engaging across all the channels someone chooses to use is as, or even more, efficient or pleasant than using single channels in isolation.

Predictive analytics It encompasses a variety of statistical techniques from data mining, predictive modeling, and machine learning that analyze current and historical facts to make predictions about future or otherwise unknown events.

In business, predictive models exploit patterns found in historical and transactional data to identify risks and opportunities. Models capture relationships among many factors to allow assessment of risk or potential associated with a particular set of conditions guiding decision making for candidate transactions.

Procurement It is the process of finding and agreeing to terms and acquiring goods, services, or works from an external source, often via a tendering or competitive bidding process. Procurement generally involves making buying decisions under conditions of scarcity. If sound data is available, it is good practice to make use of economic analysis methods such as cost-benefit analysis or cost-utility analysis.

Return on investment (ROI) It is the ratio between net profit over a period and cost of investment. A high ROI means the investment's gains compare favorably to its cost. As a performance measure, ROI is used to evaluate the efficiency of an investment or to compare the efficiencies of several different investments. In economic terms, it is one way of relating profits to capital invested.

Six Sigma It is a set of techniques and tools for process improvement. It was introduced by American engineer Bill Smith while working at Motorola in 1980. Jack Welch made it central to his business strategy at General Electric in 1995. A Six Sigma process is one in which 99.99966% of all opportunities to produce some feature of a part are statistically expected to be free of defects.

Smart manufacturing It is a broad category of manufacturing that employs computer-integrated manufacturing, high levels of adaptability, and rapid design changes, digital information technology, and more flexible technical workforce training. Other goals sometimes include fast changes in production levels based on demand, optimization of the supply chain, efficient production, and recyclability. In this concept, a smart factory has interoperable systems, multi-scale dynamic modeling and simulation, intelligent automation, strong cyber security, and networked sensors.

Smart cities   A smart city is an urban area that uses different types of electronic Internet of things and sensors to collect data and then use insights gained from that data to manage assets, resources, and services efficiently. This includes data collected from citizens, devices, and assets that is processed and analyzed to monitor and manage traffic and transportation systems, power plants, utilities, water supply networks, waste management, crime detection, information systems, schools, libraries, hospitals, and other community services.

Spend analytics   It is the process of collecting, cleansing, classifying, and analyzing expenditure data with the purpose of decreasing procurement costs, improving efficiency, and monitoring controls and compliance. It can also be leveraged in other areas of business such as inventory management, contract management, complex sourcing, supplier management, budgeting, planning, and product development.

Taiichi Ohno   A Japanese industrial engineer and businessman, Taiichi Ohno is considered to be the father of the Toyota Production System, which inspired lean manufacturing in the US. He devised the seven wastes as part of this system. He wrote several books about the system, including *Toyota Production System: Beyond Large-Scale Production*.

Three-dimensional printing   It is better known as, simply, 3D printing, This process builds a three-dimensional object from a computer-aided design model, usually by successively adding material layer by layer, which is why it is also called additive manufacturing unlike conventional machining, casting, and forging processes, where material is removed from a stock item (subtractive manufacturing) or poured into a mold and shaped by means of dies, presses, and hammers.

Third-party logistics (abbreviated as 3PL or TPL)   In supply chain management, it refers to an organization's use of third-party businesses to outsource elements of its distribution, warehousing, and fulfillment services. Third-party logistics providers typically specialize in integrated operations of warehousing and transportation services that can be scaled and customized to customers' needs, based on market conditions, to meet the demands and delivery service requirements for their products.

Value network It is a graphical illustration of social and technical resources within/between organizations and how they are utilized. The nodes in a value network represent people (or abstractly, roles). The nodes are connected by interactions that represent deliverables. These deliverables can be objects, knowledge, or money. Value networks record interdependence. They account for the worth of products and services. Companies have both internal and external value networks.

Value stream mapping Also known as 'material- and information-flow mapping', it is a lean-management method for analyzing the current state and designing a future state for the series of events that take a product or service from the beginning of the specific process until it reaches the customer. A value stream map is a visual tool that displays all critical steps in a specific process and quantifies easily the time and volume taken at each stage. Value stream maps show the flow of both materials and information as they progress through the process.

Warehouse management system (WMS) It is a software application designed to support and optimize warehouse functionality and distribution center management. These systems facilitate management in their daily planning, organizing, staffing, directing, and controlling the utilization of available resources, to move and store materials into, within, and out of a warehouse, while supporting staff in the performance of material movement and storage in and around a warehouse.

Working capital (abbreviated as WC) It is a financial metric which represents the operating liquidity available to a business, organization, or other entity, including governmental entities. Along with fixed assets such as plant and equipment, working capital is considered a part of operating capital. Gross working capital is equal to current assets. Working capital is calculated as current assets minus current liabilities. If current assets are less than current liabilities, an entity has a working capital deficiency.

INDEX

Printed in the United States
By Bookmasters